Barcode in Back

MW01122383

# A Foster Christmas

## Also by Norm Foster

# A Foster Christmas

## Norm Foster

Ethan Claymore

Dear Santa

The Christmas Tree

Bob's Your Elf

Playwrights Canada Press
Toronto • Canada

PLAYWRIGHTS CANADA PRESS
*The Canadian Drama Publisher*
215 Spadina Ave., Suite 230, Toronto, Ontario, Canada, M5T 2C7
phone 416.703.0013    fax 416.408.3402
orders@playwrightscanada.com • www.playwrightscanada.com

Playwrights Canada Press acknowledges the financial support of the Government of Canada through the Canada Book Fund and the Canada Council for the Arts, and of the Province of Ontario through the Ontario Arts Council and the Ontario Media Development Corporation for our publishing activities.

Cover photo © Jupiterimages and Hemera Technologies
Cover design by Blake Sproule
Production editor: MZK

Library and Archives Canada Cataloguing in Publication

Foster, Norm, 1949-
A Foster Christmas / Norm Foster.

Four plays.
ISBN 978-0-88754-887-1

1. Christmas plays, Canadian (English).  I. Title.

PS8561.O7745F64 2009        C812'.54        C2009-905618-6

First edition: October 2010
Printed and bound in Canada by AGMV Marquis, Montreal

# ❄ Table of Contents ❄

# Ethan Claymore

*Ethan Claymore* was first produced at The Grand Theatre in London, Ontario, October 30 to November 13, 1998, with the following cast and production team:

| | |
|---|---|
| ETHAN CLAYMORE | Ric Reid |
| MARTIN CLAYMORE | David Ferry |
| DOUGLAS McLAREN | Jerry Franken |
| TERESA PIKE | Catherine Fitch |
| YOUNG ETHAN | Scott Wilkinson |
| YOUNG MARTIN | Nik Longstaff |

Director: Miles Potter
Set & Costume designer: Peter Hartwell
Lighting designer: Erica Hassell
Stage manager: Lauren Snell
Assistant stage manager: A. Naomi Wiebe

**Characters**

| | |
|---|---|
| ETHAN CLAYMORE | Thirty-eight years old |
| MARTIN CLAYMORE | Forty-three years old |
| DOUGLAS McLAREN | In his fifties or sixties |
| TERESA PIKE | In her thirties |
| YOUNG ETHAN | Twelve years old |
| YOUNG MARTIN | Sixteen years old |

# ACT ONE Scene One

*Time: The present. Monday, December 21st.*

*Place: The home of Ethan Claymore.*

*It is a farmhouse. The kitchen and the living areas are contained in the same space. There is a kitchen table and chairs in the room, and a woodstove for heat. There is also an easel in the room on which sits a canvas, and there is a small table with paints nearby. There is a door leading outside, and a window, which looks out onto the front yard.*

*As the lights come up there is no one onstage. It is night. The room is dark. We see a figure pass by the window. It is DOUGLAS McLaren, a man in his fifties. He wears a winter coat over his overalls. He knocks on the door.*

**DOUGLAS** *(off)* Ethan!!? Ethan!!

> *He knocks again.*

It's December the twenty-first, now open up!!

> *He cups his hands around his eyes and peers in through the window.*

I know you're in there, Ethan, now open this door before I break it down!!

> *ETHAN Claymore enters from his bedroom. He is tying a robe around himself as he moves.*

**ETHAN**    What the.... Who's there?

**DOUGLAS** Never mind who's here. Just open this door!

**ETHAN**    Douglas? *(He moves to the door and opens it.)* Douglas, what are you doing?

> *DOUGLAS marches into the room.*

**DOUGLAS** Ethan, it's December the twenty-first.

**ETHAN**    What?

**DOUGLAS** It's December the twenty-first.

**ETHAN**    December the twenty-first.

**DOUGLAS** Yes.

**ETHAN**    Well, thank you, Douglas. Are you spreading this news to all the neighbours, or just the ones you suspect of being without calendars?

**DOUGLAS** Ethan, I've come to inform you that your period of mourning is officially over.

**ETHAN**    My what?

**DOUGLAS** December the twentieth, five years ago, your Jenny passed on, rest her soul.

**ETHAN**     Yes. And?

**DOUGLAS** And you've been mourning that sweet thing for five years now. Well, it's over, Ethan. Enough is enough. For five years I've watched you work this place all by yourself, never visiting your neighbours, never attending any social functions, never going out at all for that matter. Not to mention the fact that you haven't celebrated Christmas for five years. Good heavens, Ethan, you don't even put up a Christmas tree anymore. Well, it's December the twenty-first, and that is going to change starting today. Starting right now!

**ETHAN**     Douglas, it's one a.m....

**DOUGLAS** Yes, it is. And it's over. Today, you are returning to the world of the living. And I'm the one who is going to lead you there.

**ETHAN**     You?

**DOUGLAS** Me. Douglas Aloysius McLaren. Now, I've taken the liberty of drawing up a list of things we have to do. *(He takes a piece of paper out of his pocket.)*

**ETHAN**     Douglas...

**DOUGLAS** Uh-uh-uh!! You just hold your tongue until I'm through. Now, sit down. Sit, sit.

>           *ETHAN sits.*

All right, now. Number one. We're going to get you some new clothes. I am sick and tired of seeing you in those godforsaken overalls of yours. How do you expect to make an impression when you walk around looking like Li'l Abner every day?

**ETHAN**     What about you? You wear overalls.

**DOUGLAS** I'm married. I don't have to impress anyone.

**ETHAN**     And who do I have to impress?

**DOUGLAS** Teresa Pike. Number two on my list. I'm going to introduce you to her.

**ETHAN**     Who?

**DOUGLAS** Teresa Pike. She moved to Gladden's Head four months ago. She's a teacher at the public school.

**ETHAN**     Never heard of her.

**DOUGLAS** Well of course you haven't, you donkey's ass. You never go out. You never talk to anyone. How would you hear anything!?

**ETHAN**     Donkey's ass? Isn't that redundant?

**DOUGLAS** Never mind! You're going to meet her, and you're going to like her!

**ETHAN** Douglas, I don't want to meet...

**DOUGLAS** Uh-uh-uh!! It's been decided. There's no point in arguing. That brings me to number three. You work too much, Ethan. You need to consort more. Fraternize. And to that end, you're going to start coming with me to Robert Ludlow's Fina Station, and you're going to sit around there and talk to me and Robert and Woody Hull and Calvin Chase.

**ETHAN** What'll we talk about?

**DOUGLAS** Nothing. Not a blessed thing. That's the whole point. That's why I go there every afternoon.

**ETHAN** So you can talk to Robert, and Woody...

**DOUGLAS** And Calvin, yes.

**ETHAN** About nothing.

**DOUGLAS** Absolutely nothing. The afternoon passes and our minds go completely unchallenged.

**ETHAN** And you enjoy this?

**DOUGLAS** I wouldn't miss it for the world. And you'll feel the same way, I guarantee it. *(looking at his list)* And finally, number four. A Christmas tree. Something to brighten up this tomb you've buried yourself in. You leave that one up to me. I won't rest until I find you the perfect Christmas tree, Ethan. A tree that'll fire up the Christmas spirit, and set you on the road to recovery. There. That's it. That's the list. You can go back to sleep now. *(He puts his list away.)*

**ETHAN** Have you been drinking, Douglas?

**DOUGLAS** I had an eggnog.

**ETHAN** Did you put anything in it?

**DOUGLAS** Half a pint of rum, if it's any of your business! Now you march yourself into that bedroom of yours and get some sleep, Ethan Claymore, because you've got a big day ahead of you, and I want you at your best. Goodnight, sir!

> *He exits.*
>
> *DOUGLAS walks by the window, glances in, and sees that Ethan hasn't moved.*

I said get to bed!

**ETHAN** All right, I'm going.

> *ETHAN exits to the bedroom. Lights down.*

## ACT ONE Scene Two

> *Time: That same morning. Monday, December 21st.*
>
> *Place: The same.*
>
> *Lights up, there is no one onstage. ETHAN enters through the door. He is wearing a winter coat over overalls, and is carrying a small basket of eggs. He puts the basket in the refrigerator, and takes one egg with him to the stove. He takes off his coat and hangs it up, then he takes out a frying pan and places it on the stove. DOUGLAS enters. He is carrying some mail. He stands there as if expecting ETHAN to say something. ETHAN turns around and sees him.*

**ETHAN**     Oh, good morning, Douglas.

**DOUGLAS** I suppose you didn't see me out there.

**ETHAN**     Out where?

**DOUGLAS** Walking up the road to your house here.

**ETHAN**     Oh, were you walking up my road?

**DOUGLAS** Yes, I was walking up your road.

**ETHAN**     Well, no, I guess I didn't see you.

**DOUGLAS** And you didn't hear me call to you either, I suppose.

**ETHAN**     Did you call to me?

**DOUGLAS** Several times. "Morning Ethan!" I said. Then I said it again. *(He waves.)* "Morning Ethan! I got your mail for you!" You see that there? That's a wave. I was calling and waving.

**ETHAN**     Well I'm sorry, Douglas. Someone disturbed my sleep last night and this morning my senses aren't as sharp as they could be.

> *Ethan takes the mail from DOUGLAS.*

**DOUGLAS** You're welcome.

**ETHAN**     So, what can I do for you... Aloysius?

**DOUGLAS** Oh, so, you remember my visit last night, do you?

**ETHAN**     Yes, I do. Do you?

**DOUGLAS** Yes, quite vividly. And did you think about what I said?

**ETHAN**     Douglas, you had a snootfull last night, and you were babbling. Now, I'm willing to forget about it if you are. *(looking at the mail)* Look at these bills. This is the favour you do me? Bringing my bills in for me? Some friend. Final notice, it says. Look at that.

**DOUGLAS** Are you falling behind?

**ETHAN**     No, I started behind. I just haven't caught up yet.

**DOUGLAS** What is it? Business not good?

**ETHAN**     Oh it's about the same, Douglas. The problem is my expenses keep going up. And my truck died yesterday and now I've got to get that fixed too. Would you like some breakfast?

**DOUGLAS** No, we haven't got time for breakfast. We have to get over to Erdie's Menswear. They open in fifteen minutes.

**ETHAN**     Erdie's Menswear?

**DOUGLAS** *(takes his list out of his pocket)* Number one on my list. New clothes.

**ETHAN**     Douglas, I am not getting any new clothes. I can't afford new clothes.

**DOUGLAS** Well, how are you going to impress Teresa Pike looking like a... an egg farmer?

**ETHAN**     I am an egg farmer.

**DOUGLAS** But you don't have to look like one. I mean, look at me, I grow corn. Do I look like a corn-grower?

**ETHAN**     No, you don't.

**DOUGLAS** You see?

**ETHAN**     You look like an egg farmer. *(He opens a piece of mail.)*

**DOUGLAS** Ethan, cut it out. Now, you're going to make an impression on this woman whether you like it or not.

**ETHAN**     No, I'm not, Douglas, because I won't even be meeting the woman. *(He starts to read the letter.)*

**DOUGLAS** Well, that's where you're wrong, Ethan. You see here? Number two on my list. Introduce Ethan to Teresa Pike. Well, on my way over here this morning I stopped by the school and had a word with Miss Pike. I explained to her that it was a custom in this area for the new teachers to introduce themselves around to all the parents, and that it seems that everyone's met her except for this friend of mine named Ethan Claymore. Mind you, I didn't tell her that you weren't a parent, but that's a small point. Well, she was very apologetic and she promised that she'd stop by after school this afternoon and make your acquaintance. Now, I can be here to help break the ice if you like, but personally I think that my presence would be an intrusion, and Lord knows I've never been one to intrude.

> *Ethan doesn't respond.*

Ethan? Did you hear what I said?

**ETHAN**     *(not listening)* Uh... I'm sorry, Douglas, no I didn't.

**DOUGLAS** Ethan, what's the matter?

**ETHAN**     Nothing. Uh…. It seems my brother's passed away.

**DOUGLAS** Your brother?

**ETHAN**     Yes. Martin.

**DOUGLAS** I didn't even know you had a brother. You've never spoken about a brother.

**ETHAN**     Well, he's been selling cars back home for the past… I don't know… fifteen years. It says he had a heart attack. Forty-three years old.

**DOUGLAS** Ethan, I'm sorry.

**ETHAN**     No, that's okay. We weren't very…. I mean, I haven't talked to him in a long time.

*(He puts the letter away.)* Now, what were you saying?

**DOUGLAS** Uh… nothing. It can wait.

**ETHAN**     Are you sure?

**DOUGLAS** Yes, yes. Is there anything I can do, Ethan?

**ETHAN**     No.

**DOUGLAS** I mean, Caroline and I, we're just down the road. If there's anything you need, just call us.

**ETHAN**     Douglas, I'm fine. Really.

**DOUGLAS** Well, all right. I'd better go then.

**ETHAN**     You just got here.

**DOUGLAS** I know, but I'd better go. I'll leave you to your thoughts.

**ETHAN**     You're not going to pester me about your list anymore?

**DOUGLAS** Tomorrow. There'll be plenty of time for pestering tomorrow. For now, I'll just get out of your way.

**ETHAN**     Oh Douglas, wait.

> *He moves to the refrigerator and takes out the basket of eggs.*

Take these to Caroline, would you? She said she was going to make egg bread today.

> *He gives the basket to DOUGLAS.*

**DOUGLAS** Oh, certainly. Thank you. I'll see you tomorrow then. Goodbye, Ethan.

> *DOUGLAS exits. ETHAN picks up the letter. We flashback to Ethan's childhood. Two boys, YOUNG MARTIN and YOUNG ETHAN, enter from Ethan's bedroom. Martin is sixteen, Ethan is eleven. Martin carries a pair of skates and a hockey stick.*

**YOUNG
ETHAN**     Come on, Martin, why can't I play too?

**YOUNG
MARTIN**     Because you can't, Nancy. You can't even skate. You'll just get in the way.

**YOUNG
ETHAN**     I can too skate.

**YOUNG
MARTIN**     Not like us you can't.

**YOUNG
ETHAN**     *(moving to ETHAN at the counter)* Dad, Martin won't let me play hockey with him.

**ETHAN**     Well he's right, Ethan. Those boys are big. You'll get in the way and you'll get hurt.

**YOUNG
ETHAN**     Dad, please. I'll be careful.

**ETHAN**     No, Ethan.

**YOUNG
ETHAN**     Please. I'll just stay off to the side until somebody passes it to me. I'll stay away from everybody. Please.

**ETHAN**     Ethan…

**YOUNG
ETHAN**     Please?

**ETHAN**     *(beat)* All right, just this once then.

**YOUNG
ETHAN**     Yayyy! I'll get my stuff.

*He exits to the bedroom.*

**YOUNG
MARTIN**     Aw, Dad, does he have to??

**ETHAN**     Just this once, Martin. As soon as he sees how hard it is to play with you fellas, he won't ask again. And you look out for him, you hear? Don't let the other boys knock him around any. I don't want him coming back here in tears. All right?

**YOUNG
MARTIN**     Yeah.

**ETHAN**     And don't stick him in goal either.

**YOUNG
MARTIN**     Yeah.

ETHAN     And after you've finished playing, I want you to work on your stops and starts. That scout's going to be at the game tomorrow and I want him to see what a good two-way player you are. Okay?

YOUNG
MARTIN     Yep.

ETHAN     Good boy.

YOUNG
MARTIN     I can't believe he's coming all the way from Toronto just to see me.

ETHAN     Well he's an old friend of mine, and that's what friends do for each other. Family and friends, Martin. The two most important things in life. Remember that.

YOUNG
MARTIN     How could I forget? You say it every other day.

ETHAN     And for good reason. But now, he's not gonna recommend you to a junior team just because he's a friend. You're going to have to impress him, all right?

YOUNG
MARTIN     I will.

          *YOUNG ETHAN enters from the bedroom carrying a pair of skates and a hockey stick.*

YOUNG
ETHAN     Okay, I'm ready.

YOUNG
MARTIN     Come on then.

ETHAN     Martin?

          *He grabs a banana from the counter and tosses it to YOUNG MARTIN.*

Here. You need your potassium for those young muscles.

YOUNG
MARTIN     Thanks, Dad.

          *YOUNG MARTIN exits.*

ETHAN     Ethan? You be careful now.

YOUNG
ETHAN     I will.

ETHAN     And if they try to put you in goal, say no.

YOUNG
ETHAN     Okay. *(He starts for the door.)*

ETHAN     Oh, Ethan, have you finished the painting for your mother yet?

**YOUNG
ETHAN**     Not yet.

**ETHAN**     Well, you'd better get a move on. Christmas will be here before you know it.

**YOUNG
ETHAN**     I will.

> *YOUNG MARTIN enters again.*

**YOUNG
MARTIN**     Come on, Nancy, let's go.

> *YOUNG MARTIN exits.*

**YOUNG
ETHAN**     Dad, Martin called me Nancy again.

**ETHAN**     Just go, Ethan. Go on.

**YOUNG
ETHAN**     Goodbye, Dad. Wait up, Martin!!

> *He exits. Lights down.*

## ACT ONE Scene Three

> *Time: Later that afternoon*
>
> *Place: The same.*
>
> *Lights up to reveal ETHAN standing at his easel, painting. There is a knock on the door. ETHAN opens the door. TERESA Pike is there. She is a woman in her thirties. She carries a bakery box and an old briefcase.*

**TERESA**     Mr. Claymore?

**ETHAN**     Yes.

**TERESA**     Hello. I'm Teresa Pike. I'm a teacher at the public school.

**ETHAN**     How do you do?

**TERESA**     Fine, thank you. I'm afraid I've been remiss in getting around to meeting you.

**ETHAN**     Meeting me?

**TERESA**     Yes. Do you have a moment?

**ETHAN**     Uh... sure. Come in.

**TERESA**     Thank you.

*She enters.*

I know I should have come here long before now, but I was unaware of the local custom. Oh, here. This is for you.

*She hands him the box.*

It's a cherry pie. I stopped off at Mrs. Bright's Bakery on my way.

ETHAN    *(takes the pie)* Thank you.

TERESA    I moved out here from the city, and in the city of course it would be difficult to get around and visit all of the parents, but with the smaller classes here, I guess it's more feasible.

ETHAN    The parents?

TERESA    Yes. And I quite like the idea actually. Getting around to the children's homes will give me a chance to see their environments. Now, I haven't met any Claymore children yet. I teach grades four and five. Yours must be in a lower grade, is that right?

ETHAN    My what? My children?

TERESA    *(notices the painting material)* Oh, someone in the family paints. That's nice. I think it's good for a child to be exposed to art. It provides a nice balance to the academic side of things. So, who's the artist? Your wife? You?

ETHAN    Uh… no Miss Pike, my wife died five years ago.

TERESA    Oh, I'm sorry. I didn't know.

ETHAN    No, that's all right.

TERESA    So, it's you then? You're the artist.

ETHAN    Hmm? Oh yes, well, I try. Miss Pike, I think there's been a misunder—

TERESA    *(looking at the canvas)* Oh, that's very good. That's exceptional.

ETHAN    *(beat)* Really?

TERESA    Yes. It has heart. Depth. It's very reminiscent of Bierstadt's landscapes.

ETHAN    Bierstadt? You think so?

TERESA    Oh, yes.

ETHAN    I do like Bierstadt.

TERESA    Well, you can see the influence.

ETHAN    Did you study art?

TERESA    Books. I read books. I haven't got cable. Yes, that's very good indeed.

ETHAN      Thank you.

TERESA     So, how many children do you have?

ETHAN      *(looking at his painting)* None.

TERESA     None?

ETHAN      None. I was having trouble with the shading in the background, but it's starting to come around I think.

TERESA     I thought you had children.

ETHAN      Uh... no.

TERESA     Well... are they grown up? Moved away?

ETHAN      No. Never had any. Can I get you a cup of tea? It's already made.

TERESA     Uh.... Well, there's no point in my staying if you don't have children.

ETHAN      Oh.

TERESA     I thought you had children.

ETHAN      No.

TERESA     Because that's why I came. That's why I brought the pie.

ETHAN      My neighbours have children. I could call them over.

TERESA     No, no. That's fine.

ETHAN      They're nice kids. At least that's what I hear.

TERESA     No. Never mind.

ETHAN      So, will you have some tea?

TERESA     Uh... well... it's already made you say?

ETHAN      Yes.

TERESA     Well, as long as I'm here anyway, all right then.

ETHAN      Good. *(He moves to get the tea.)*

TERESA     Why did I think you had children?

ETHAN      No idea.

TERESA     Would you like to have children?

> *There is a pause as ETHAN looks at TERESA.*

I mean, someday. With someone.

ETHAN      Well, if I was going to have children, "with someone" would be a good way.

TERESA    No, I was just thinking that if you were going to have children, I would probably be their teacher one day, that's all.

ETHAN    You plan to be here for a while then, do you?

TERESA    Well, I like it here, yes. It's away from everything.

*DOUGLAS bursts in the door.*

DOUGLAS Ethan?

*He sees TERESA.*

Oh, Miss Pike. You're here already.

TERESA    *(to DOUGLAS)* You. You told me he had children.

DOUGLAS No, I didn't. No, I said you should get around to meet all the parents. And I said my friend here hadn't met you yet. You must've assumed from that somehow, that he had children.

*(to ETHAN)* Ethan, I'm sorry, I forgot that I set this up. And then when I remembered, I rushed over as quickly as I could, but... Miss Pike, I'm afraid you're going to have to leave.

ETHAN    Douglas, no...

DOUGLAS No, Ethan, it's all right. It's my mess. I'll clean it up. Miss Pike, Ethan's just suffered a loss in the family so this might not be a good time.

TERESA    *(to ETHAN)* I thought your wife died five years ago.

DOUGLAS No, not his wife. His brother. He just got word today.

TERESA    Oh, I'm sorry.

ETHAN    No, that's all right.

DOUGLAS *(to TERESA)* So, if it's all right with you, maybe we can reschedule.

TERESA    Certainly. Reschedule what?

DOUGLAS Your meeting.

ETHAN    Douglas, I was just going to pour some tea.

DOUGLAS Oh, no thank you, Ethan. None for me. Miss Pike? I'll see you home.

ETHAN    Douglas, Miss Pike is staying for tea.

DOUGLAS She is?

ETHAN    Yes.

DOUGLAS Oh. *(beat)* Why?

ETHAN    Because I invited her to.

DOUGLAS You did?

**ETHAN**   Yes.

**DOUGLAS** Oh. Oh!! Well, then I've interrupted something. I'm sorry.

**TERESA**   No, we were just talking about having children.

**DOUGLAS** *(beat)* Well, then there's no point in my staying around is there? I'd only be in the way. Well, I'll just run along then. Sorry to barge in like that. Miss Pike, you have a nice day.

**TERESA**   You too.

**DOUGLAS** Thank you. I will. Ethan.

**ETHAN**   Goodbye, Douglas.

> *DOUGLAS exits and closes the door.*

Have a seat, please.

**TERESA**   Thank you.

> *She moves to the table and sits.*
>
> *The door opens and DOUGLAS enters again and speaks to TERESA.*

**DOUGLAS** By the way, those are just his work clothes.

**ETHAN**   Douglas?

**DOUGLAS** *(to TERESA)* I mean, when he puts his mind to it, he can slick up real nicely.

**ETHAN**   Douglas...

**DOUGLAS** Goodbye now.

> *DOUGLAS exits.*

**ETHAN**   You'll have to excuse Douglas. He thinks he's helping me.

**TERESA**   Helping you what?

**ETHAN**   Well... get back into socializing I guess.

**TERESA**   You haven't been socializing?

**ETHAN**   Well, not according to Douglas I haven't been. But this farm keeps me pretty busy. I've got two thousand hens out there that I have to tend to, and I'm the only employee I've got so there's not much time for anything else. And what extra time I do find, I spend right there at the easel.

**TERESA**   Uh-huh. So, your brother... he really died?

**ETHAN**   That's what it said in the letter.

**TERESA**   The reason I ask is that you don't seem terribly upset.

**ETHAN**   Well, Martin and I were very different. We didn't speak much.

*He moves down with the teapot and cups on a tray.*

Here we go. Just help yourself to the milk and sugar.

*He sets the tray down on the table.*

**TERESA**  Thank you.

**ETHAN**  *(moves to his easel)* So it reminds you of Bierstadt, huh? That's interesting.

**TERESA**  Yes. Did you paint that from a photograph? There are certainly no mountains like that around here.

**ETHAN**  No, it's from memory. I grew up near the mountains.

**TERESA**  Oh.

**ETHAN**  I moved to Gladden's Head with my wife just after we got married.

**TERESA**  Why Gladden's Head?

**ETHAN**  Well, we just wanted to get away I guess. Jenny was a sculptor and… well, we had this idea that we were going to live the idyllic artisan's life.

**TERESA**  And did you?

**ETHAN**  No, we found out, much to our surprise, that you have to have money to live, so we borrowed some and bought this egg farm.

**TERESA**  How did your wife die, Mr. Claymore?

**ETHAN**  Leukemia. And please, call me Ethan.

**TERESA**  All right. Ethan.

**ETHAN**  And enough about my life. What about you? What brings you to Gladden's Head?

**TERESA**  The job.

**ETHAN**  That's it?

**TERESA**  That's it. You go where the work is.

**ETHAN**  And where's home?

**TERESA**  Ottawa.

*Awkward pause.*

The nation's capital.

**ETHAN**  *(beat)* The Parliament Buildings are there.

**TERESA**  That's the place. *(beat)* So, can you really slick up nicely?

**ETHAN**  What? Oh! Well, I don't know. It's been so long since I slicked up for anything.

**TERESA**   Well, if you're looking for an excuse to, the school's having a parent's Christmas party Wednesday night. You could slick up and go to that.

**ETHAN**   But I'm not a parent.

**TERESA**   Well, I could probably sneak you in.

**ETHAN**   But Wednesday, that's the day after tomorrow.

**TERESA**   So?

**ETHAN**   *(looking at his clothes)* Well, it's just that I haven't got any... I mean, it's short notice.

**TERESA**   Well, it was just a thought.

**ETHAN**   Uh-huh. A party. I haven't been to a party in... I don't know how long.

**TERESA**   Five years?

**ETHAN**   About that.

**TERESA**   Well, if you're not busy that night, it should be fun. Rumour has it Paul Campbell's going to show us his appendicitis scar.

**ETHAN**   Well, that does sweeten the pot. Thanks. I'll think about it.

**TERESA**   Well, I'd better get going. I've got a lot of tests to mark tonight.

> *She stands.*

**ETHAN**   Oh, okay.

**TERESA**   Thank you very much for the tea.

**ETHAN**   You're welcome.

**TERESA**   And uh... well, maybe we'll see you at the party.

**ETHAN**   Well, I don't know about that, but, we'll see.

> *He opens the door for her.*

And thanks for the pie, Miss Pike.

**TERESA**   Teresa.

**ETHAN**   Teresa. Good.

**TERESA**   Goodbye.

**ETHAN**   Bye now.

> *TERESA exits. ETHAN closes the door. He goes to his painting and looks at it. The door opens and DOUGLAS enters.*

**DOUGLAS** Well??

**ETHAN**   Douglas? Back so soon?

**DOUGLAS** I never left. I was waiting in the chicken barn.

**ETHAN**  Waiting for what?

**DOUGLAS** To see how it went. Now, how'd it go? Did you like her?

**ETHAN**  She's fine.

**DOUGLAS** Fine? Just fine?

**ETHAN**  She's fine.

**DOUGLAS** Well what did you talk about, besides having children?

**ETHAN**  We weren't talking about having children. We were talking about children in general. We were making small talk. I mean, she was only here a few minutes.

**DOUGLAS** Oh. So, you didn't hit it off?

**ETHAN**  What do you mean, hit it off?

**DOUGLAS** Well, sparks? Were there any sparks?

**ETHAN**  No, Douglas, there were no sparks.

**DOUGLAS** Any smoke? Because you know, where there's smoke there's fire.

**ETHAN**  No. No smoke.

*He picks up the tray of tea and moves it to the counter.*

**DOUGLAS** No heat of any kind?

**ETHAN**  No, Douglas.

**DOUGLAS** Well, then you just weren't trying, Ethan. You just plain weren't trying. Darn it, how am I supposed to help you if you won't put forth the effort?

**ETHAN**  I don't know, Douglas.

**DOUGLAS** Well, I'm not giving up. No sir. Douglas McLaren is no quitter. And you're about to find that out.

*DOUGLAS opens the door and starts to leave.*

**ETHAN**  Douglas?

**DOUGLAS** *(stopping)* What?

**ETHAN**  What time does Erdie's Menswear stay open till tonight?

**DOUGLAS** Erdie's? Six o'clock, I think.

**ETHAN**  Thanks.

**DOUGLAS** Why? Are you thinking of…. You're not thinking of…

**ETHAN**  I'm thinking about it.

**DOUGLAS** Oh. Good. Well if you can't make it by six, I could call Erdie and tell him to stay open a bit longer.

**ETHAN**     No, that's okay. I can make it.

**DOUGLAS** Yessir!! One more thing I can cross off my list! Oh, I'm working on the Christmas tree, Ethan. I got a line on a good tree lot over in Vicker's Rock. I'll head over there tomorrow morning.

**ETHAN**     That's thirty miles away.

**DOUGLAS** I told you, Ethan. I'm not buying just any tree. I'm buying you the perfect tree.

**ETHAN**     Well, you do what you like, Douglas, but I'm telling you, it won't get put to much use here.

**DOUGLAS** Oh, we'll see about that. *(He starts to leave and then returns.)*

Oh, by the way, Ethan, tomorrow afternoon we're going to the Fina station.

**ETHAN**     We're what?

**DOUGLAS** Number three on my list. Remember?

**ETHAN**     Oh, right. Sit around and talk about nothing.

**DOUGLAS** That's right.

**ETHAN**     Well, we'll see how busy I am.

> *He has his back to DOUGLAS as he works at the counter.*
>
> *MARTIN Claymore enters through the open door. He is wearing a business suit. DOUGLAS cannot see him, and ETHAN isn't looking. MARTIN looks around the room, then wanders over to the easel and looks at the painting.*

**DOUGLAS** Never mind that. You're going. I've already told the boys you'll be there. They're very excited. New blood and all that. All right?

**ETHAN**     We'll see.

**DOUGLAS** Good. I'll pick you up at two. So long, Ethan.

> *DOUGLAS exits and closes the door.*

**MARTIN**     Still painting I see, Nancy.

**ETHAN**     *(turning around)* What? *(beat)* Oh, my God. Oh my God. Martin? Is that you?

**MARTIN**     Been a long time, Ethan.

**ETHAN**     Martin? I... I thought you were dead.

**MARTIN**     I am.

**ETHAN**     You are what?

**MARTIN**     Dead. Very much so.

**ETHAN**     No, I mean, I got a letter saying that you had died. It said you had a heart attack.

**MARTIN**     I did have a heart attack.

**ETHAN**     No, it said you died.

**MARTIN**     I did die.

**ETHAN**     No, it said you were dead.

**MARTIN**     I am dead. Exactly what part of this don't you understand?

**ETHAN**     I don't understand any of this.

**MARTIN**     All right, let me try and explain. Last week, I was showing a young couple this used Riviera on the car lot. The young lady—quite a striking woman—the young lady says to me can they take it for a test drive. And I says, "Sure. Just let me go inside and get the…"

**ETHAN**     Get the what?

**MARTIN**     Nothing. That's as far as I got. Next thing I know, I'm down on one knee and I'm hanging on to the Riviera's bumper. The young woman asks me if I'm all right, and I say, "I'll be fine." Those were my last words. "I'll be fine."

**ETHAN**     So, you did have a heart attack.

**MARTIN**     I sure did. Hurt like hell. I thought I was gonna die. Turns out I was right.

**ETHAN**     Wait a minute. What are you saying?

**MARTIN**     I'm trying to tell you that I'm dead, Ethan. And I'm not happy about it either. I could've sold that Riviera.

**ETHAN**     All right, Martin, what is this? What are you trying to pull?

*The door opens and DOUGLAS enters again.*

**DOUGLAS** Ethan, you'll want me to come with you to Erdie's of course. I mean, I have a pretty keen eye for fashion as you can tell, so you'll probably want me to be there, right?

*ETHAN doesn't answer.*

Ethan?

**MARTIN**     Hey, Douglas? Over here.

**DOUGLAS** Ethan, are you going to answer me or not?

**MARTIN**     Douglas?? Yoo-hoo? *(He moves to the door.)*

**DOUGLAS** Well, fine then. If you don't want me to come just say so. You don't have to ignore me. *(He turns to leave.)*

**ETHAN**      Douglas?

**DOUGLAS** What?

**ETHAN**      You can't see him?

**DOUGLAS** See who?

**ETHAN**      Him. Right there.

**DOUGLAS** *(looking around)* Right where?

**ETHAN**      Right there. There.

**MARTIN**      Forget it, Ethan. He'll think you're crazy.

**DOUGLAS** What are you, crazy?

**MARTIN**      Too late.

**DOUGLAS** Now you call me when you're ready to go to Erdie's, all right? And have a nap. You're seeing things that aren't there.

*DOUGLAS exits and closes the door.*

**ETHAN**      He didn't see you.

**MARTIN**      That's right.

**ETHAN**      No, I mean, he didn't see you at all. Like you were invisible.

**MARTIN**      Now you're catching on.

**ETHAN**      Oh, now wait a minute, wait a minute, wait a minute.

**MARTIN**      It's true, Ethan.

**ETHAN**      No, it's not.

**MARTIN**      I know it's a shock, but it's true.

**ETHAN**      You're a ghost?

**MARTIN**      No, they don't call us ghosts. We're shadow beings.

**ETHAN**      Shadow beings?

**MARTIN**      Yeah, in life we were human beings, and at this stage we're only shadows of our human selves, so we're shadow beings.

**ETHAN**      We? You mean there are more of you? *(He looks around.)*

**MARTIN**      Don't worry. I'm the only one you'll see.

**ETHAN**      I'm asleep, aren't I? I dozed off and I'm dreaming.

**MARTIN**      I'm afraid not.

**ETHAN**      No, I am. I've been working hard lately. I'm just tired, that's all.

**MARTIN**      Take that spoon and stick it in the teapot, Ethan.

**ETHAN**      What?

**MARTIN**    Take the spoon there and stick it in the teapot.

**ETHAN**    Why?

**MARTIN**    Just do it.

>*ETHAN sticks the spoon into the teapot.*

**ETHAN**    All right, now what?

**MARTIN**    Just wait a second. *(beat)* Okay, take it out.

>*ETHAN takes the spoon out.*

Now, touch the back of your hand with the spoon.

>*ETHAN does it. The spoon burns.*

**ETHAN**    Ow!!

**MARTIN**    Well, you're not dreaming. I guess I'm here.

**ETHAN**    But why? What are you doing here?

**MARTIN**    Well, I'm not sure. I don't know a whole lot about my assignment yet. I just know it's going to happen here.

**ETHAN**    Assignment?

**MARTIN**    Yeah. I'm here to set somebody on the right path or something. Apparently, when you've wronged somebody in life, you have to do something good for someone after you die. Which is pretty unfair if you ask me, telling you the rules after the game is over.

**ETHAN**    Who did you wrong?

**MARTIN**    Ethan, I was a car salesman.

**ETHAN**    I can't believe this.

**MARTIN**    You can't believe it? A heart attack at forty-three years old. I thought only the good died young. *(looking at the painting)* This is back home, isn't it?

**ETHAN**    Hmm?

**MARTIN**    The painting. That's back home. The mountains, the Bedwell's house… *(beat)* And the pond.

**ETHAN**    Yeah.

**MARTIN**    Hmm. *(He moves across the room to the kitchen counter.)*

Ooh, bananas. Dad turned me into a banana addict. Remember that? "Eat your bananas, Martin. Your muscles need the potassium." He didn't tell me that too much potassium could also lead to heart trouble. Man, I ate about ten of those things every day until the day I died. I couldn't get enough.

**ETHAN**    Go ahead. Have one.

MARTIN   No.

ETHAN   Well, how about a sandwich? Can I fix you a sandwich?

MARTIN   Ethan, we don't eat.

ETHAN   You don't?

MARTIN   Don't eat, don't drink. Nothin'. Don't need to. Even if I wanted to, I couldn't pick it up.

ETHAN   Why not?

MARTIN   I'm in the spirit world. I'm not a physical presence. I can't touch anything here.

ETHAN   Does that mean you can't... move something?

MARTIN   What do you mean?

ETHAN   You know? Levitate something.

MARTIN   Why do people think that as soon you die, you turn into David Copperfield?

ETHAN   So, what's it like in the spirit world?

MARTIN   Drafty.

ETHAN   Drafty?

MARTIN   Yeah, it's chilly. But then I suppose somebody else is monopolizing all the heat.

ETHAN   I still can't believe this is happening.

MARTIN   So how's the egg farming business?

ETHAN   Hmm? Oh, good. Good.

MARTIN   No, it's not.

ETHAN   Yes, it is.

MARTIN   Ethan, I know.

ETHAN   You do?

MARTIN   Of course I do. So, what's the problem?

ETHAN   Well, I've got two thousand hens out there laying one egg a day. That's not enough to cover my costs anymore.

MARTIN   So get more hens.

ETHAN   Well if I do that I've got to build another barn, buy more equipment. I haven't got the money for that.

MARTIN   One egg a day, huh? Bunch of underachievers if you ask me. Well, not unlike yourself.

**ETHAN**      I've done all right.

**MARTIN**      The bank's gonna put a lien on your farm, Ethan. That doesn't sound all right to me.

**ETHAN**      The bank's not putting a lien on my farm. Who told you that?

>      *MARTIN just shrugs knowingly.*

They're putting a lien on my farm?

**MARTIN**      The notice went out in the mail on Friday. You'll get it tomorrow.

**ETHAN**      Well, what does it say?

**MARTIN**      *(thinking)* Well, let's see now. "Dear Mr. Claymore. It has come to our attention that…"

**ETHAN**      Not the whole letter. Just the important part.

**MARTIN**      It says you've got until the end of the month to come up with five thousand dollars, or you lose the farm. You got five thousand dollars, Ethan?

**ETHAN**      No.

**MARTIN**      I know you don't.

**ETHAN**      I'll bet you're happy about that, aren't you, Martin?

**MARTIN**      Doesn't matter to me one way or the other.

**ETHAN**      When was the last time we talked?

**MARTIN**      Beats me.

**ETHAN**      It was fourteen years ago. Just before Jenny and I moved out here. Do you remember what you said to me then?

**MARTIN**      Can't say as I do.

**ETHAN**      You said you hoped I didn't mess up Jenny's life like I messed up yours. You made me feel guilty about that my whole life.

**MARTIN**      I wound up selling cars, Ethan. Don't talk to me about how you felt. How do you think I felt?

**ETHAN**      But it wasn't my fault.

**MARTIN**      Hold it, hold it. *(He looks around as if he's heard something.)* I gotta go.

**ETHAN**      What? Go where?

**MARTIN**      I don't know. I just know I have to go.

**ETHAN**      Why?

**MARTIN**      They want to talk to me.

ETHAN      Who?

MARTIN     The ones who hand out the assignments.

ETHAN      And who are they?

MARTIN     Three women.

ETHAN      Women?

MARTIN     Yeah. And boy, are they giving me a hard time.

ETHAN      Well, are you coming back?

MARTIN     Oh, yeah. I'll be back. See you later. *(starts for the door)*

ETHAN      Well, when? When are you coming back?

MARTIN     I don't know. Soon. Why?

ETHAN      Well, I don't want you scaring me again like you did this time.

MARTIN     Fine. I'll give you some warning next time.

ETHAN      Wait, wait. How are you going to leave?

MARTIN     What do you mean?

ETHAN      Well, do you disappear? Do you walk through walls?

MARTIN     No, I don't walk through walls. That freaks me out. Makes me feel like Casper.

ETHAN      So how do you leave?

           *The door opens on it's own, as if by magic.*

MARTIN     All right, so we know a few tricks. So long, Nancy. I'll be in touch.

           *MARTIN exits. The door closes by itself. After a beat, YOUNG ETHAN enters through the front door in a panic.*

YOUNG
ETHAN      Dad!! Dad!!

ETHAN      What is it, Ethan?

YOUNG
ETHAN      Dad, you've got to come to the pond. It's Martin.

ETHAN      Martin? What happened?

YOUNG
ETHAN      I didn't mean it, Dad. It wasn't my fault. Honest. Jim Bedwell pushed me.

ETHAN      All right, Ethan, calm down and tell me what happened.

YOUNG
ETHAN      I was playing defence—they tried to put me in goal, but I said no— so I was playing defence and Martin was coming in and I was just going to

get out of his way because I didn't want to get hurt, but Jim Bedwell pushed me in front of him.

**ETHAN**     In front of Martin?

**YOUNG ETHAN**     Yes. And we got all tangled up and Martin went down funny on his leg.

**ETHAN**     What do you mean funny?

**YOUNG ETHAN**     Well it got all twisted up like, underneath him. And now he can't walk.

**ETHAN**     All right, let's go. *(He moves to get his coat.)*

**YOUNG ETHAN**     I didn't mean it, Dad. It's not my fault. Martin keeps saying it's my fault, but it was Jim Bedwell.

**ETHAN**     All right, Ethan, I know. But I told you you shouldn't play with those boys. They're too big.

**YOUNG ETHAN**     Jim Bedwell's a jerk.

**ETHAN**     Yes, he is. He always has been.

**YOUNG ETHAN**     But why? How does he get like that?

**ETHAN**     It's inherited, son. His father's a jerk. Maybe his grandfather too. I never met the man.

　　　　　*ETHAN and YOUNG ETHAN exit. Lights down.*


## ACT ONE Scene Four

　　　　　*Time: The next afternoon. Tuesday, December 22nd.*

　　　　　*Place: The same.*

　　　　　*As the scene opens, ETHAN and DOUGLAS enter. They are wearing their winter coats. ETHAN takes his coat off and hangs it up. DOUGLAS stares at him as he does this.*

**ETHAN**     All right, Douglas, what is it?

**DOUGLAS** What's what?

**ETHAN**     Well you didn't say a word the whole way home, and for you, that's not normal. Now, what's wrong?

**DOUGLAS** What's wrong?

**ETHAN**  Yes, what's wrong?

**DOUGLAS** All right, Ethan, I'll tell you what's wrong. I take you to the Fina Station for a nice afternoon of friendly chit-chat with some friends of mine. A favourable way to pass the time I think. Always has been. Why should today be any different? And what do you do? You start talking about ghosts and reincarnation and life after death.

**ETHAN**  So?

**DOUGLAS** Ethan, I told you, the rules are very clear. We talk about nothing at the Fina Station. Nothing. We talk about Harvey Pelletier's rebuilt transmission. Gordie Washburn's new shed. Sue Ann Tuckey's planter's warts. We don't talk about life after death at the Fina! You scared the heck out of those fellas. Poor Calvin darn near fell off his orange crate. And Woody? When you started in about the spirit world, I thought he was gonna choke on his Mountain Dew.

**ETHAN**  I didn't say anything wrong. I was just talking about whatever popped into my head.

**DOUGLAS** Well, stop it. You keep those thoughts to yourself. Those fellas won't sleep for weeks now. They'll be afraid to close their eyes. And what the heck is a shadow being?

**ETHAN**  Well, it's what they call a...

**DOUGLAS** Never mind! I don't want to know.

**ETHAN**  All right, next time I won't talk about anything of substance.

**DOUGLAS** If there is a next time. Those boys might not want you coming back again. I mean, Robert got up to use the washroom four times while you were there. He never goes that much. I think you upset his regulatory system.

**ETHAN**  All right, I'm sorry. Would you like a coffee?

**DOUGLAS** Coffee?

**ETHAN**  Yes.

**DOUGLAS** Coffee. Well, you know it's pretty cold out there, Ethan. It might be better if I had something to warm me up for the trip home.

**ETHAN**  You live a hundred yards away.

**DOUGLAS** Well, it is bitter cold.

**ETHAN**  You've got your truck.

**DOUGLAS** Ethan, are you going to offer me a rum or not?

**ETHAN**  Of course I am. I just wanted to see you squirm.

> *ETHAN goes to the kitchen and takes out a bottle of rum. He pours a drink for DOUGLAS.*

**DOUGLAS** Oh, I went over to Vicker's Rock to find you a Christmas tree this morning, but they didn't have what I'm looking for. And on the way back I checked into a lot in Hartsburg, but they were scrawny things, so I think after supper I'll head down to Newton. Myrna Pollock's cousin Travis has got a tree lot down there next to his scrapyard.

**ETHAN** You're going to buy a Christmas tree from a scrap dealer?

**DOUGLAS** Well, now don't sell Travis short now. He's got quite a nativity scene set up down there. He's got an old rusted out DeSoto for a manger, and three little garden gnomes for the wise men. It's a real attraction. Speaking of attractions, the whole town is talking about your date with Miss Pike tomorrow night.

**ETHAN** My what?

**DOUGLAS** Your date. The party at the school.

**ETHAN** Miss Pike and I don't have a date.

**DOUGLAS** Well, you bought those new clothes yesterday.

**ETHAN** I bought those new clothes because it was number one on your list.

**DOUGLAS** Oh, that's why.

**ETHAN** That's right. And I'm going to the party because you said I work too much. You said I should consort more. Fraternize, remember?

**DOUGLAS** Oh, I see.

**ETHAN** There's no date involved here. I'm going alone.

**DOUGLAS** Of course you are.

**ETHAN** I am.

**DOUGLAS** In that truck of yours that doesn't work, I suppose.

**ETHAN** No, I was going to ask you and Caroline for a ride.

**DOUGLAS** Oh.

**ETHAN** So can I have one?

**DOUGLAS** Of course, of course.

**ETHAN** Thank you.

**DOUGLAS** Unless you get a better offer before then.

> *ETHAN hands DOUGLAS his glass of rum.*

Ah, there we go. Thank you. You're not having one?

**ETHAN** No.

**DOUGLAS** But it's the festive season. You don't expect me to toast the season alone, do you?

**ETHAN** You don't want it then?

**DOUGLAS** That's not what I said.

**ETHAN** Well, if you don't want to drink alone I'll take it back.

> *He reaches for the glass.*

**DOUGLAS** Uh-uh-uh! As long as you've poured it I'll force myself. But just this once. Season's greetings, Ethan.

> *He raises his glass in a toast then drinks.*

**MARTIN** *(off, in a ghostly howl)* Oooooooohhh. Oooooohhhh!!!

**ETHAN** What was that?

**DOUGLAS** What?

**ETHAN** That noise. Did you hear that?

**DOUGLAS** Oh, I'm sorry. I didn't pass gas, did I?

**ETHAN** No, no, no. Listen.

**MARTIN** *(off)* E-e-e-ethan Claymore!!!

**ETHAN** There. That.

**DOUGLAS** I didn't hear anything.

> *The door swings open and MARTIN enters.*

**MARTIN** How ya doin?

**DOUGLAS** Ah. Must've been the wind you heard.

> *DOUGLAS moves to close the door.*

**ETHAN** *(to MARTIN)* What are you doing?

**DOUGLAS** I'm closing the door. It's cold out there.

**ETHAN** *(to MARTIN)* I said what are you doing?

**DOUGLAS** *(loudly)* I'm closing the door! It's cold out there!

**MARTIN** So, is that better?

**DOUGLAS** *(after closing the door)* There that's better.

**ETHAN** *(to MARTIN)* Better than what?

**DOUGLAS** Well, better than leaving it open.

**ETHAN** *(to DOUGLAS)* Uh… yes, thank you. That's much better.

**DOUGLAS** You're welcome.

**MARTIN** You said you wanted some warning.

**ETHAN**     *(to MARTIN)* I what?

**DOUGLAS** You're welcome. Are you all right?

**ETHAN**     *(to DOUGLAS)* Uh… yes, yes. Fine.

**DOUGLAS** Good. Come on, Ethan, let's sit for a bit. There's nothing like enjoying the company of friends during the yuletide. *(He moves to a chair.)*

**ETHAN**     *(to DOUGLAS)* No!

**DOUGLAS** What?

**ETHAN**     No, you can't sit.

**DOUGLAS** Why not?

**ETHAN**     Uh… because I have things to do. And if you stay I'll never get to them.

**DOUGLAS** What things?

**ETHAN**     I… have to clean the manure out of the chicken barn.

**MARTIN**    Oh, good one.

**DOUGLAS** Now?

**ETHAN**     Yes. Right now.

**DOUGLAS** But I haven't finished my drink yet.

**ETHAN**     Take it with you.

**DOUGLAS** What?

**ETHAN**     Take it with you.

**DOUGLAS** But it'll be finished in five minutes.

**MARTIN**    Let the man sit.

**ETHAN**     *(to MARTIN)* Oh be quiet.

**DOUGLAS** What?

**ETHAN**     Not you.

**DOUGLAS** Not me what?

**ETHAN**     Nothing. Please Douglas, just go.

**DOUGLAS** Are you throwing me out?

**ETHAN**     No, I'm not throwing you out. Of course not.

> He takes DOUGLAS by the arm and leads him up to the door.
> The door swings open.

**DOUGLAS** You know you oughta get the latch on that door fixed.

**ETHAN**     *(to MARTIN)* Will you cut that out?

**DOUGLAS** Cut what out? I'm just giving you some friendly advice.

**ETHAN** Yes, well, thank you, Douglas. I'll get it fixed right away.

**DOUGLAS** After you clean up the manure you mean.

**ETHAN** Right. (*in a friendly way*) Now, if you don't get out of here, Douglas Aloysius McLaren, I won't get anything done.

**DOUGLAS** Well, all right.

> *He steps outside the door with his drink in his hand.*

You go to it, Ethan.

> *He stops outside and turns back to ETHAN.*

But I swear. I've never seen a man so anxious to get to a pile of chicken...

> *The door swings closed before DOUGLAS can finish.*

**ETHAN** So you're back.

**MARTIN** That I am.

**ETHAN** I was hoping you were just a dream.

> *He goes to the counter and pours himself a rum.*

**MARTIN** No such luck.

**ETHAN** So did you find out about your assignment?

**MARTIN** No, they're swamped right now. It's a busy season for redemption I guess. They just told me to sit tight and they'll get back to me. So, you got your notice from the bank.

**ETHAN** Yeah, got it this morning, just like you said I would. (*He picks up a letter.*)

**MARTIN** It's amazing how I know all this stuff, huh? I tell you, if I'd had this knowledge while I was still alive, I would've been a rich man. I'd know which horse was going to win at the track, what the lottery numbers would be.

**ETHAN** Well, it's nice to see that you'd use that knowledge to help mankind.

**MARTIN** Yeah, right. And what did mankind ever do to help me? Gave me a torn up knee and heart disease. Remind me to send it a thank-you card.

**ETHAN** You know, I would've thought that dead people wouldn't be bitter like that.

**MARTIN** Wouldn't be bitter? We're dead. We're all bitter! I met a man here who lived till he was a hundred and two. He thinks he got shortchanged.

**ETHAN** Well, I would think that you'd be remorseful.

**MARTIN**    Ethan, I died and I lost a Riviera sale. It's been a bad week. Get the door.

**ETHAN**    What?

*There is a knock on the door*

**MARTIN**    Man, this is fun.

**ETHAN**    *(moving to the door)* And don't you distract me.

**MARTIN**    I won't say a word.

**ETHAN**    Don't even breathe.

**MARTIN**    I haven't for over a week now.

*ETHAN opens the door. TERESA Pike is there.*

**TERESA**    Hello.

**ETHAN**    Oh, Teresa. Hi.

**TERESA**    Hi.

**MARTIN**    Hi.

**TERESA**    How are you today?

**ETHAN**    Fine.

**MARTIN**    I'm dead on my feet.

**TERESA**    Cold weather we're having.

**ETHAN**    Yes, it is.

**MARTIN**    Ethan, can't you take a hint? Invite her in.

**ETHAN**    Uh... would you like to come in?

**TERESA**    All right. But just for a moment.

*TERESA enters. ETHAN closes the door.*

I just stopped by to ask you something.

**ETHAN**    Oh? And what's that?

**TERESA**    Well I heard that your truck was broken down, and I was wondering if you'd be needing a ride tomorrow night.

**MARTIN**    Oh, she likes you.

**ETHAN**    Uh... well, actually Douglas McLaren and his wife have already offered me a ride.

**TERESA**    Oh.

**MARTIN**    What?!

**TERESA**    Well, all right then.

MARTIN   Are you out of your mind?

TERESA   So you won't be needing one then?

MARTIN   Yes, he will.

ETHAN    No, I won't.

MARTIN   Yes, you will.

ETHAN    No, I won't!

TERESA   Fine.

MARTIN   Ethan, can I see you over by the stove please? *(He moves into the kitchen.)*

TERESA   Well, that's all I stopped by for then.

MARTIN   Ethan?

TERESA   Just wanted to make sure you weren't stranded here.

MARTIN   Ethan? Now!

ETHAN    *(to TERESA)* Uh… could you hold on for just a second, please? I have to check on something in the oven.

TERESA   Oh, certainly.

> *ETHAN moves to the kitchen. He opens the oven and looks in.*

MARTIN   Ethan, who would you rather ride with? This woman here who, for some reason, seems to like you? Or Uncle Jed and Granny next door? I mean, do you think she goes around offering rides to everybody who has no transportation? Man, if I could kick your butt right now I would. *(looking skyward)* Come on, let me kick him once! Just once!

> *ETHAN closes the oven and moves back to TERESA.*

Say yes, Ethan. Or I'll haunt you for the rest of your life.

TERESA   Everything okay?

ETHAN    Yes, perfect.

TERESA   Cooking supper, are you?

ETHAN    Yes.

TERESA   Funny, I don't smell anything. It doesn't even look like the oven's on.

ETHAN    No, well, it's steak tartar.

MARTIN   Oh, nice save.

ETHAN    You know, Teresa, maybe I will accept your kind offer of a ride.

TERESA   Oh. All right.

**MARTIN**   There you go.

**TERESA**   I'll pick you up on my way to get Mr. and Mrs. Olmstead.

**ETHAN**   Mr. and Mrs. Olmstead?

**TERESA**   Yes, they both have failing eyesight and they can't drive. And then we have to pick up Harvey Pelletier. He's having his transmission rebuilt. You see, the school thought we should offer rides to anyone who doesn't have transportation.

**ETHAN**   Oh, I see.

**TERESA**   So, I'll be by tomorrow, about seven-thirty?

*TERESA moves to the door. ETHAN opens it for her.*

**ETHAN**   Seven-thirty. Good.

**TERESA**   Good. Well, see you then.

**ETHAN**   Goodbye.

**MARTIN**   *(waving)* Tartar.

*ETHAN closes the door.*

**ETHAN**   You knew, didn't you?

**MARTIN**   Of course I knew. I know everything.

**ETHAN**   You're not a very nice person in death either, are you?

**MARTIN**   Hey, is that any way to talk to your brother who loves you?

**ETHAN**   I have to go. *(He gets his coat.)*

**MARTIN**   Go? Go where?

**ETHAN**   The manure is piling up.

*He opens the door.*

It's piling up in the chicken barn too.

*He exits.*

**MARTIN**   *(to himself)* The kid never could take a joke.

*YOUNG MARTIN enters from the bedroom. He is limping badly. He sits in the chair. YOUNG ETHAN enters, wearing a winter coat and carrying a small artist's canvas and a book bag.*

**YOUNG ETHAN**   How ya feeling?

**YOUNG MARTIN**   How do you think I'm feeling? I'll never play hockey again, that's how I'm feeling.

YOUNG
ETHAN    Well, at least you don't have to stay in the hospital over Christmas. You should be happy about that.

YOUNG
MARTIN    Leave me alone.

YOUNG
ETHAN    Martin, it wasn't my fault.

YOUNG
MARTIN    Get lost.

YOUNG
ETHAN    *(He puts his canvas into the bag.)* You want me to bring you something back?

YOUNG
MARTIN    Where are you going?

YOUNG
ETHAN    I have to take my painting of Mom over to Mr. Hoffman's to get it framed. If I don't get it over there today it won't be ready for Christmas. So do you want anything?

YOUNG
MARTIN    No.

YOUNG
ETHAN    I can go to the library and get you a book if you want.

YOUNG
MARTIN    I said no.

YOUNG
ETHAN    Okay. *(checking his coat pockets)* Where are my gloves?

YOUNG
MARTIN    How should I know where your stupid gloves are?

YOUNG
ETHAN    They must be in my room.

> *He exits to his room.*

> *YOUNG MARTIN gets up from the chair. He takes the canvas out of Young Ethan's bag. He bends it in half and throws it into the woodstove, then sits again. YOUNG ETHAN enters, putting his gloves on. He picks up his bag.*

YOUNG
ETHAN    Well, see ya later.

> *YOUNG MARTIN doesn't answer. YOUNG ETHAN starts for the door. When he gets to the door, he stops.*

Martin, I'm really sorry you hurt yourself so bad. I mean it. I wish it was me who got hurt 'cause I don't care about hockey like you do. I don't care if can play or not and I know you do. I'm really sorry, okay?

*YOUNG MARTIN doesn't answer.*

Okay, Martin?

*YOUNG ETHAN exits. YOUNG MARTIN stares straight ahead. MARTIN stands behind him and stares out.*

*Lights down.*

*End Act One.*

## ACT TWO Scene One

*Time: Wednesday, December 23rd.*

*Place: The same.*

*As the scene opens there is no one onstage. The door to the home swings open and MARTIN enters. The door swings closed behind him.*

**MARTIN**  *(to himself)* What a lousy party that was. No alcohol, no dancing. How do the Amish do it?

*There is a crash of thunder and a flash of lightning. MARTIN looks up.*

It was a joke! I'm joking! Boy, for a person who gave us the ostrich, you don't have much of a sense of humour. By the way, I've been meaning to ask you, what happened to this light you're supposed to see when you're dying? You know, I heard you're supposed to walk towards the light. Well, I didn't see any light. I was fumbling around in the dark there for a good twenty minutes.

*MARTIN wanders over and looks at the painting.*

I wish I could go back there. No second chances I guess, huh? *(Beat; as he waits for an answer.)* No, I didn't think so.

*YOUNG MARTIN enters from the bedroom. He limps to a chair and sits. The door opens and YOUNG ETHAN rushes in.*

**YOUNG ETHAN**  Dad? Dad!

*ETHAN enters from the bedroom.*

**ETHAN**  What's wrong?

**YOUNG ETHAN**  Dad, I lost my painting.

**ETHAN**  What?

**YOUNG ETHAN**  My painting of Mom. It's gone.

**ETHAN**  Gone? How could you lose it?

**YOUNG ETHAN**  I don't know. I put it in my bag and I thought I zipped it shut, but maybe I didn't. I don't know. And when I was running to Mr. Hoffman's, it must've fallen out I guess.

**ETHAN**  Oh, Ethan.

**YOUNG
ETHAN**  Dad, what am I gonna do? That was my Christmas present for Mom.

**ETHAN**  All right, all right. *(He gets his coat and puts it on.)*

We'll find it. Which way did you go? Past the pond, or through the woods?

**YOUNG
ETHAN**  The woods.

**ETHAN**  All right, we'll just retrace your steps then.

**YOUNG
ETHAN**  But, I already looked.

**ETHAN**  Well, we'll look again.

**MARTIN**  *(to YOUNG MARTIN)* Tell them.

**ETHAN**  Now you went straight there, did you? You didn't go anywhere else first?

**YOUNG
ETHAN**  No, I went straight there.

**ETHAN**  All right then. We'll find it.

**MARTIN**  *(to YOUNG MARTIN)* Tell them.

**ETHAN**  Martin, we'll be right back. Come on, Ethan.

> *YOUNG ETHAN and ETHAN exit. MARTIN moves to YOUNG MARTIN.*

**MARTIN**  Get up. Call them back.

> *YOUNG MARTIN doesn't hear.*

Get up, you coward!

> *YOUNG MARTIN gets out of the chair and moves to the front door. He opens it.*

Call them. Go on. They can still hear you.

> *YOUNG MARTIN says nothing.*

Call them!

> *MARTIN steps outside and yells:*

Dad! Ethan! Come back! I took the painting! It was me! Dad!?

> *YOUNG MARTIN turns away from the door. He moves towards the bedroom. MARTIN turns and looks at him from outside.*

I hate you.

*A flash of lightning and a crash of thunder. The door swings closed.*

*The door opens and ETHAN enters. He is wearing the clothes he purchased at Erdie's. Nice slacks and a shirt under his winter coat. He looks outside as he enters.*

**ETHAN**     *(to himself)* Awfully cold weather for thunder and lightning.

*(He looks around the room.)* Martin... Martin, are you here? Are you anywhere?

*He hangs up his coat.*

*MARTIN enters from the bedroom.*

**MARTIN**     What is it?

*ETHAN is startled.*

**ETHAN**     Geez! Don't do that. It's bad enough when real people sneak up on you, let alone a... someone like you.

**MARTIN**     You were going to say ghost, weren't you?

**ETHAN**     Well to my mind, that's what you are. That's what we've been told all our lives. Dead people who come back are ghosts.

**MARTIN**     And I suppose you're too old to change, huh?

**ETHAN**     Don't talk to me about changing, Martin. Even dying couldn't change you.

**MARTIN**     So, where's your date?

**ETHAN**     What?

**MARTIN**     Your date. The woman.

**ETHAN**     She wasn't my date.

**MARTIN**     Whatever. Where is she?

**ETHAN**     She's on her way home.

**MARTIN**     What?

**ETHAN**     She's on her way home. She dropped me off and went home.

**MARTIN**     You didn't invite her in?

**ETHAN**     No.

**MARTIN**     Well, what's the matter with you? She wanted you to invite her in.

**ETHAN**     She did?

**MARTIN**     Of course she did. She likes you.

**ETHAN**     But she only gave me a ride tonight because it was school policy.

MARTIN    The school policy was an excuse to give you a ride, you bonehead. Man, you make me mad sometimes. You just don't catch on, do you?

ETHAN.    Catch on to what?

MARTIN    You're naive, Ethan. You always have been. You don't know it when somebody likes you, and you don't know it when somebody's trying to hurt you. You make me sick.

ETHAN    What are you getting so angry about?

MARTIN    Forget it. What's the point?

ETHAN    *(beat)* You mean she does like me.

MARTIN    Never mind. Get the door.

        *DOUGLAS enters.*

DOUGLAS  Ethan?

MARTIN    Oh, right. He never knocks.

ETHAN    Hello, Douglas.

DOUGLAS  Where's your date?

ETHAN    She wasn't my date. And she's on her way home.

DOUGLAS  What, you didn't invite her in?

MARTIN    You see?

ETHAN    No, Douglas, I didn't invite her in.

DOUGLAS  Why not? She likes you.

ETHAN    Well, I didn't know she liked me.

DOUGLAS  She gave you a ride tonight, didn't she?

ETHAN    I thought the ride was school policy. I didn't know the school policy was an excuse to give me a ride.

DOUGLAS  I thought everybody knew it was an excuse. Everybody at the party knew.

ETHAN    Well, I missed the signal I guess.

DOUGLAS  Gee, you'd have to be a bonehead to miss that signal.

MARTIN    I'm starting to like this guy.

DOUGLAS  Anyway, I've got something for you, Ethan. *(He takes a cheque out of his pocket.)*

ETHAN    What's that?

DOUGLAS  Caroline and I want you to take this. You can pay us back whenever you want. No rush.

**ETHAN**   Five thousand dollars?

**DOUGLAS** Now, it's not charity. That's a loan. I don't want you to think we're taking pity on you.

**ETHAN**   How did you know I needed five thousand dollars?

**DOUGLAS** Everybody knows.

**ETHAN**   But, this is bank business. Isn't that supposed to be confidential?

**DOUGLAS** How long have you lived here, Ethan? When one of us is in trouble, we're all in trouble, and that makes it everybody's business, you oughta know that.

**ETHAN**   Well I appreciate this, Douglas, but...

**DOUGLAS** Uh-uh-uh. Never mind. I'm not doing it for you anyway. I'm doing it for me. I mean, if you're forced out of here there's no telling what kind of neighbours I'll get next. *(He moves to the kitchen area.)*

They might be a bunch of snobs, or moochers, or God forbid, teetotalers.

> *He takes the bottle of rum out of the cupboard and pours himself a drink.*

Oh, by the way, I'm still working on that Christmas tree, Ethan. I went down to Travis Pollock's tree lot yesterday but his selection was limited. Got to see that nativity scene though so it wasn't a total loss. And then this afternoon I tried a couple of lots over in Kelly's Junction but they didn't have the perfect tree either. Tomorrow though. I'll get you one tomorrow for sure. Cheers.

> *He drinks.*

**ETHAN**   Douglas...

> *There is a knock on the door.*

**MARTIN**   Oh, now who could that be?

> *ETHAN opens the door. TERESA is there.*

**TERESA**   Hello, Ethan, I'm sorry to bother you. I haven't caught you at a bad time I hope.

**ETHAN**   No.

**TERESA**   Good. I can't believe this.

**ETHAN**   What's wrong?

**MARTIN &**
**DOUGLAS** Invite her in!!

**ETHAN**   Uh... come in, please.

**TERESA**   Oh, thank you.

MARTIN     *(to DOUGLAS)* Kid's as thick as a brick.

> *TERESA enters. ETHAN closes the door.*

ETHAN     So, what's the problem?

TERESA     Well... oh, hello, Douglas.

DOUGLAS Miss Pike.

TERESA     Well, the strangest thing just happened. I pulled out onto the highway there and my car died.

ETHAN     What?

TERESA     Just quit for no reason. Like someone turned off the ignition or something.

DOUGLAS Sounds like the alternator to me.

MARTIN     That'd be my guess too.

TERESA     So, I was wondering if I could use your phone to call a tow truck?

DOUGLAS Oh, no need for that. I'll give you a ride home, Miss Pike. We can look after that car of yours tomorrow.

MARTIN     Yeah, it'll probably start tomorrow.

TERESA     Oh, well, that's very kind of you, Douglas.

ETHAN     That might not be a good idea, Douglas. I mean, you have been drinking.

DOUGLAS Oh, right. Well, I'll tell you what then. I'll call Caroline and she can drive you home, Miss Pike.

TERESA     Thank you. That's very kind.

> *DOUGLAS moves to the phone.*

MARTIN     Here's a better idea, Doug.

DOUGLAS Actually, I've got a better idea. I'll walk over and get Caroline.

ETHAN     Why? Why not just phone her?

DOUGLAS Well... because.

ETHAN     Because why?

DOUGLAS Because I don't want to.

ETHAN     Why not?

DOUGLAS Because if I walk over, it'll take longer and it'll give you two some time alone. Now, isn't that a good idea?

MARTIN     It's a great idea.

DOUGLAS See you in a bit.

> *DOUGLAS exits.*

**ETHAN**    *(to TERESA)* I'm sorry about that.

**TERESA**    It seems the good people of Gladden's Head are determined to get us together somehow.

**ETHAN**    Oh, you've noticed, have you??

**TERESA**    Oh, yes. I guess no one thinks that a person can be alone in this world. Everybody's got to be attached, you know?

**ETHAN**    Yeah.

**TERESA**    Especially around Christmastime. Nobody likes to think that someone's going to spend Christmas alone.

**MARTIN**    Offer her a seat.

**ETHAN**    *(to MARTIN)* I was going to.

**TERESA**    Going to what?

**ETHAN**    Spend Christmas alone.

**TERESA**    Yes, me too.

**ETHAN**    Would you like to sit?

**TERESA**    Oh, thank you.

> *TERESA sits. There is a pause.*

**ETHAN**    Well.

**MARTIN**    *(to ETHAN)* Hello? What about a drink? Something to take the chill off?

**ETHAN**    Would you like a drink? Rum and eggnog?

**TERESA**    Oh, all right. That'd be nice. But only if you're having one.

**ETHAN**    Sure, I'll have one.

> *He moves to the cupboard to get the drinks.*

Too bad about your car.

**TERESA**    Yes. *(beat)* It really did die on me. I mean, I didn't make that up just to... you know... so I could come back here and...

**ETHAN**    No, I believe you. I'm sure it did die. *(looking at MARTIN)* In fact, I know it did. *(beat)* So, you're spending Christmas alone. You've got no family to spend it with?

**TERESA**    No, my parents spend every Christmas in Florida. They invited me to come down, but Christmas in Florida wouldn't seem like Christmas to me.

**ETHAN**    No brothers or sisters?

**TERESA**   No, I'm an only child I'm afraid.

**ETHAN**   Well, now, there's a lot to be said for being an only child.

**MARTIN**   Watch it.

**TERESA**   Well, I always wished I had a sister.

**MARTIN**   I did have a sister. Right, Nancy?

**TERESA**   It would've been nice to have had someone to share my childhood with. An older sister that I could learn from. Look up to. I think we would've been very close.

*ETHAN gives TERESA her drink.*

Thank you. So, you and your brother, you weren't close?

**ETHAN**   Not really.

**TERESA**   Why not?

**ETHAN**   *(beat)* I don't know. Things happened. *(changing the subject)* So, you've never been married?

**TERESA**   No.

**ETHAN**   Well, that's surprising. An attractive, intelligent woman like you. No man's ever proposed to you?

*TERESA doesn't answer.*

**MARTIN**   Oh-oh. Sore spot.

**ETHAN**   *(to TERESA)* I'm sorry. Is that a sore spot?

**MARTIN**   Isn't that what I just said?

**ETHAN**   *(to MARTIN)* Do you mind?

**TERESA**   No, I don't mind. I'm over it now. I was engaged. We were supposed to be married in June, but... well, I got cold feet. I realized that he wasn't the one I wanted to spend the rest of my life with. I guess I'm looking for the perfect man. Like Douglas and your Christmas tree I guess.

**ETHAN**   You know about that, huh?

**TERESA**   The whole town knows.

**ETHAN**   So, you broke off the engagement?

**TERESA**   Actually, I broke off the wedding.

**ETHAN**   You what?

**TERESA**   Yeah. Right there at the church.

**ETHAN**   You got as far as the church?

**TERESA**   Oh, further. In fact, all the way to the part where the minister says "If anyone here knows of any reason why these two should not be joined together, let them speak now or forever hold their peace."

**ETHAN**   And then what?

**TERESA**   Well, I put up my hand.

**ETHAN**   You didn't.

**TERESA**   I did. I mean, I had to. I looked around and saw that nobody else was going to. And it would've been unfair to me and to my fiancé to go through with it, so I thanked everyone for coming, walked out of the church, flagged down a cab, and here I am.

**ETHAN**   Wow.

**TERESA**   Yeah, wow. But, like I say, I'm pretty much over it now.

*She takes a big drink of her rum and eggnog.*

I understand it's taken you quite a while to get over your wife's death. That's what I'm told anyway.

**ETHAN**   Uh... well...

**TERESA**   Oh, I'm sorry. I shouldn't have brought that up.

**ETHAN**   No, that's okay. Jenny and I were... well, we were very much in love.

I don't think you ever get over feelings like that.

**TERESA**   No, I guess not. But you don't stop living either. I mean, I don't think you do. I don't know. I've never been in that position.

**MARTIN**   Come on, Ethan, make your move. The old man's gonna be back soon.

**ETHAN**   *(beat)* So... uh... do you enjoy teaching at the school here?

**TERESA**   Oh, yes. Very much. The people are very friendly here.

**ETHAN**   Yes, they are, aren't they?

**TERESA**   Yes.

**ETHAN**   Very friendly.

**TERESA**   *(beat)* And you? You enjoy living here?

**ETHAN**   Yeah. Yeah.

**MARTIN**   Oh man, this is killing me all over again.

**TERESA**   *(She stands.)* All right, look, we haven't got much time. Douglas is going to be back here soon, and I was just wondering if you'd like to have Christmas dinner at my house?

*Beat; as ETHAN looks at MARTIN.*

ETHAN       Uh...

MARTIN      Hey, I didn't make her do it. This is her idea.

TERESA      Well?

ETHAN       Uh... Christmas dinner?

TERESA      Yes, at my house.

ETHAN       With you?

TERESA      Well, I was planning on being there.

ETHAN       Well, uh... I don't know.

MARTIN      *(looking up)* Come on, just one kick in the butt. Please!

TERESA      All right, if you don't want to, that's okay. I didn't mean to put you on the spot. I'm sorry.

ETHAN       No, I'd like to.

TERESA      You would?

ETHAN       Yes. I'd like that very much.

MARTIN      Well, hallelujah!

TERESA      Well, good. All right then.

ETHAN       Good.

> *There is an awkward pause.*

TERESA      Oh, what the heck!

> *She moves forward and gives ETHAN a quick kiss.*

ETHAN       *(beat)* More eggnog?

MARTIN      Oh, yeah. That's her way of asking for more eggnog.

> *The door opens and DOUGLAS enters.*

DOUGLAS     All right, Miss Pike. We're all set.

TERESA      Oh, all right. Good.

DOUGLAS     You two have a nice chat?

TERESA      Yes.

ETHAN       Yes.

DOUGLAS     Uh-huh. Would you like more time? There's no rush.

ETHAN       Just take the lady home, would you, Douglas?

DOUGLAS     Sure. Sure.

> *TERESA moves to the door.*

**TERESA**     Well, goodnight. Again.

**ETHAN**      Yes, goodnight.

**TERESA**     See you soon.

*She exits.*

**DOUGLAS** (*to TERESA as he follows her out*) How soon? Do you know how soon?

*DOUGLAS exits.*

**MARTIN**     Well, looks like your troubles are over, huh?

**ETHAN**      Why?

**MARTIN**     Well, you've got a date for Christmas dinner. You've got your five thousand dollars. You're set.

**ETHAN**      (*picking up the cheque*) I can't take this.

**MARTIN**     Why not?

**ETHAN**      Douglas and Caroline aren't doing much better than I am. This is probably all the money they've got.

*He tears up the cheque.*

**MARTIN**     What are you doing?

**ETHAN**      I'll get out of this mess on my own.

**MARTIN**     No, you won't.

**ETHAN**      Then I'll go bankrupt. Whatever. I'm not going to take a friend's money. Dad used to say family and friends are the two most important things in life, remember? Well, at this point, I don't have any family to count on and I'll be damned if I'm going to jeopardize my friendships.

**MARTIN**     No family, huh? What about me?

**ETHAN**      That's funny, Martin. That's very funny.

*ETHAN exits to his room.*

**ETHAN**      (*off*) Ethan?

*YOUNG ETHAN enters from Ethan's room. ETHAN follows him.*

Ethan, where are you going?

**YOUNG ETHAN**     I just want to go and look one more time.

**ETHAN**      Ethan, you've looked a hundred times already. It's gone.

**YOUNG ETHAN**     Well, maybe I'll find it this time. Maybe it's...

ETHAN     Ethan, no. It's Christmas Eve. You lost that painting days ago.

YOUNG
ETHAN     I know, but maybe if I...

ETHAN     No buts. It's gone. Now you're not going out there again. It's dark out there.

YOUNG
ETHAN     I'll take a flashlight.

ETHAN     I said no. Now that's that.

YOUNG
ETHAN     But I haven't got a present for Mom. And I told her I was making her something real special.

ETHAN     Well, I offered to give you the money to buy her something else.

YOUNG
ETHAN     No, I wanted to give her my painting.

ETHAN     Ethan, she'll understand. I promise you. The fact that you went to all that trouble to paint her portrait in the first place—that you wanted to do that for her—that'll be enough, believe me. Now, if you didn't get me a present, that'd be a different story. You did get me one, didn't you?

YOUNG
ETHAN     It's not funny, Dad. I've ruined everybody's Christmas.

ETHAN     Oh, don't be silly.

YOUNG
ETHAN     I have. I haven't got a present for Mom. I made Martin get hurt. I messed up everything.

ETHAN     No, you didn't. Martin will get over it. He just needs time.

YOUNG
ETHAN     No, he won't. He won't get over it. He hates me.

ETHAN     No. No, Martin loves you, and don't you ever forget that. You hear? I will not have that kind of talk in this house. Family and friends, Ethan. They're the most important things in life. We'll always be there for you. You understand that? Always.

*YOUNG ETHAN doesn't answer.*

Come here, son.

*YOUNG ETHAN rushes to ETHAN and hugs him.*

*Lights down.*

## ACT TWO Scene Two

> *Time: The next morning. Thursday, December 24th.*
>
> *Place: The same.*
>
> *As the scene opens, Martin is onstage. He is looking out the window.*

**MARTIN** *(to himself)* Stupid snow. *(looking up)* Don't get me wrong. It's beautiful if you like that kind of thing, but we used to hate snow when we were dealing cars. Nobody buys in the snow. All the sales guys would stand around the showroom with their thumbs up their.... With their thumbs up. *(He gives the thumbs up sign.)* "Tomorrow. We'll do better tomorrow."

> *ETHAN enters from the bedroom. He's wearing his overalls now.*

Morning, Ethan.

**ETHAN** Still here, huh?

**MARTIN** Only in spirit.

**ETHAN** No word on your assignment yet? *(He heads to the kitchen area.)*

**MARTIN** No. Listen, there's no time for breakfast this morning, Ethan. You'd better go out and check your chicken barn.

**ETHAN** What for?

**MARTIN** Well there was an awful ruckus out there last night. That's what you country folk call it, isn't it? A ruckus?

**ETHAN** What do you mean? What happened?

**MARTIN** Well, you'd better go and have a look. It sounded plum serious though.

**ETHAN** Well what is it?

**MARTIN** Just go and look, would you? Go. Go.

> *ETHAN moves to put his coat and boots on.*

**ETHAN** Well, I don't know why you can't just tell me. I mean, you know everything. Why can't you tell me?

**MARTIN** No, this is something you're gonna have to see for yourself. Now, git.

> *ETHAN exits out the front door.*

*(looking up)* So this is it, huh? After this I have to go? *(beat)* Because if you don't need me right away, I thought maybe I could stay around for Christmas morning. Would that be all right? I mean, we haven't spent Christmas morning together in a lot of years. Not that it matters that much. I just thought as long as I'm here anyway. *(beat)* All right, it does matter,

okay? Is that what you want to hear? It's only another twenty-four hours. Come on. *(beat)* Hello? Anybody? *(beat)* I'll take that as a no.

*ETHAN enters the house.*

ETHAN  What happened out there?! How could that happen?!

MARTIN  What's the matter?

ETHAN  Eggs. Eggs everywhere. There must be ten... twenty thousand of them out there.

MARTIN  Sixty.

ETHAN  Sixty? Sixty thousand eggs?!

MARTIN  That's right.

ETHAN  But, that's impossible. I've got two thousand layers. They lay one egg a day!

MARTIN  Well, they were working overtime last night.

ETHAN  But, they couldn't have. They.... They'd have to lay thirty eggs each.

MARTIN  And that they did.

ETHAN  Thirty eggs. This is incredible. Was this your doing?

MARTIN  I put in a request, yeah.

ETHAN  Oh, my God. What am I gonna do?

MARTIN  Well, you've got sixty thousand eggs out there, and at the going rate for eggs, I'd say you'll have your five thousand dollars with some to spare.

ETHAN  But my cooler's not big enough to hold sixty thousand eggs. I have to get them to the grading station today. Now.

MARTIN  Well, go.

*ETHAN rushes for the door, then rushes back.*

ETHAN  My truck's not working.

MARTIN  Wait a minute. *(beat)* Now it is.

ETHAN  It is?

MARTIN  Better than ever.

*ETHAN rushes for the door and comes back again.*

ETHAN  My truck's not big enough to carry all those eggs. I'm going to need help. Douglas! I'll call Douglas.

*He rushes to the phone.*

Thirty eggs apiece. Are those chickens gonna be all right?

**MARTIN**     Well, they'll sleep for a while.

**ETHAN**     *(to the phone)* Douglas? Douglas, I need your help. I need you to get your truck over here right now... I'll explain when you get here. You won't believe it. And call anybody else who has a truck and ask them to come too.... All right. Hurry. *(He hangs up.)* I'd better get out there and get loading.

> *He exits.*
>
> *ETHAN enters again and stands in the doorway.*

**MARTIN**     What's wrong?

**ETHAN**     ...Thanks.

**MARTIN**     Just go, would ya?

> *ETHAN exits. Lights down.*

## ACT TWO Scene Three

> *Time: That evening. Christmas Eve.*
>
> *Place: The same.*
>
> *As the scene opens, ETHAN and TERESA enter.*

**TERESA**     Well, that was quite a day.

**ETHAN**     You can say that again.

**TERESA**     I've never seen that many eggs.

**ETHAN**     Listen, thanks again for helping out. I really appreciate it.

**TERESA**     Oh, it was my pleasure. It gave me something to do today. Christmas Eve, you know. Another one of those days when you don't like to sit around by yourself.

**ETHAN**     Can I get you anything? Coffee? Tea? Hot chocolate?

**TERESA**     Ooh, a hot chocolate would be nice now.

**ETHAN**     All right.

> *ETHAN moves to the kitchen. TERESA moves to the easel and looks at the painting. ETHAN looks around the room expecting Martin to show up.*

**TERESA**     You haven't done any more work on your painting.

**ETHAN**     Uh... no, well, it's been a busy week. *(whispering)* Martin? ...Martin, are you here? Where are you?

**TERESA**     Pardon me?

**ETHAN**    Uh… nothing. I was just wondering out loud where Douglas was. He left us very mysteriously a while ago. I just wonder where he went.

*He plugs in the kettle for hot chocolate.*

**TERESA**    He went to get your Christmas tree.

**ETHAN**    What? You mean he's still on about that?

**TERESA**    Yes. He was so wrapped up in this egg mission that he forgot about it. He told me he had one more place to check and that's where he went.

**ETHAN**    That man. He's stubborn as a mule.

**TERESA**    He's a good friend.

**ETHAN**    Yes, he is.

**TERESA**    And he cares about you very much. You're lucky.

**ETHAN**    I know. What about you? Do you have any close friends in town?

**TERESA**    Not really close. Not yet. I take my time when it comes to choosing friends.

**ETHAN**    Well, if things work out, I could be one.

**TERESA**    What, a friend? Oh, no, I've got other plans for you. *(beat)* That…. That was out loud, wasn't it?

**ETHAN**    Yes.

**TERESA**    Sorry.

**ETHAN**    No, that's okay. I like a woman who says what's on her mind. Even when she doesn't know she's saying it.

**TERESA**    Oh.

**ETHAN**    I like it very much. My wife was like that. You always knew where you stood with Jenny.

**TERESA**    I see. Well, as long as you like that sort of thing, then maybe this won't be so hard for me to say.

**ETHAN**    What won't?

**TERESA**    Ethan, I… uh… I'm not an outgoing person really. Not very gregarious.

**ETHAN**    You're shy.

**TERESA**    That's exactly what I am. I'm shy. So, when it comes to starting a relationship—meeting a man, that is—well, I'm not very good at it. Oh, sure, I was engaged, but it took us forever to get to that point, and even then he was the wrong guy. I mean, I don't know how many good men I might have missed out on because I was afraid to say, "Hey, I think you're cute" or, "Hey, how about buying me a drink, tall boy?" I just can't do that. I can't. So when I met you I thought, well, this time it's going to be different.

This time, I'm going to take the initiative. So I invited you to the parents' Christmas party. I invited you to my place for Christmas dinner. I even kissed you. On the mouth, I kissed you! But gee whiz, Ethan, I can't do all the work. You're going to have pitch in here once in a while too. Now I know you've still got your wife on your mind. Maybe that's what's holding you back, I don't know. And if it is... I mean, if it's still too soon for you, then just say so and I'll back off. I'll back right off. But if it isn't—I mean, if you're interested in getting something going here then holy Hanna, do something will you?

> *She sits, worn out.*

**ETHAN**     *(beat)* I am interested.

**TERESA**     You are?

**ETHAN**     Yes.

**TERESA**     Well, what are you going to do about it?

> *ETHAN moves to TERESA. They move in for a kiss but before they can, the door opens and DOUGLAS enters. He is not happy.*

**DOUGLAS** Ethan, I've got your tree. And I don't want to hear a peep out of either one of you. Not a word, you understand?

**ETHAN**     Well, where is it?

**DOUGLAS** It's right outside.

**ETHAN**     Well, aren't you going to bring it in?

**DOUGLAS** Well of course I am, you horse's hiney. I just wanted to warn you first about keeping your smart-aleck comments to yourself. Both of you. All right?

**ETHAN**     Fine.

**TERESA**     Fine.

**DOUGLAS** Fine.

> *DOUGLAS exits and then returns with a scrawny tree on a stand.*

There. There's your Christmas tree. There's your festive pile of kindling!

**ETHAN**     What happened?

**DOUGLAS** I left it too long that's what happened. It was the last tree I could find. Oh, yeah, there's more.

> *He starts for the door.*

**ETHAN**     Well, I hope there's more.

**DOUGLAS** No, not more tree! That's it. That's the tree. All of it. I meant there's something else.

ETHAN     Oh.

> *DOUGLAS exits and returns with a cardboard box.*

DOUGLAS Here. Caroline sent some ornaments over.

> *He drops the box on the floor.*

Feliz Navidad.

> *He turns to exit.*

ETHAN     Douglas, wait.

DOUGLAS What?

ETHAN     I think it's a great tree.

DOUGLAS Well, then you're a nut.

TERESA     No, Douglas, I think it's a nice tree too. Once we dress it up, it'll look beautiful.

ETHAN     Now stay. Have some hot chocolate with us. Help us decorate it.

DOUGLAS Well, just for a while. Caroline's expecting me.

ETHAN     Just for a while then.

TERESA     Now let's see what we've got in here.

> *TERESA opens up the box of ornaments.*
>
> *DOUGLAS moves to the kitchen area with ETHAN while TERESA starts decorating the tree.*

ETHAN     Well we put in quite a day's work today, didn't we?

DOUGLAS We did that.

ETHAN     And all the people who showed up to help. I couldn't believe it.

DOUGLAS It's like I said, Ethan, when one of us is trouble, we're all in trouble. Now, can I ask you something?

ETHAN     Yes, Douglas, you can have some rum in your hot chocolate.

DOUGLAS No, it's not about that, and make it a double. No, what I want to know is, how in the heck did you get sixty thousand eggs out of two thousand chickens without a shoehorn??

ETHAN     You wouldn't believe me if I told you.

DOUGLAS No, well, try me.

ETHAN     You really want to know?

DOUGLAS Well, of course I do. Sixty thousand eggs. The entire scientific community wants to know.

ETHAN     My brother Martin did it.

**DOUGLAS** Come again.

**ETHAN**     My brother Martin. He put in a request and it was granted.

**DOUGLAS** Your brother Martin?

**ETHAN**     That's right.

**DOUGLAS** The dead brother?

**ETHAN**     Yes. He came back. He's been here since Monday.

**DOUGLAS** He came back from where?

**ETHAN**     Well, he didn't actually come back. I mean, he didn't come back to life.

**DOUGLAS** Oh, good.

**ETHAN**     No, he came here on his way to wherever you go after you die. Heaven I guess. I don't know. But he stopped in here because he was in the area for an assignment, which he didn't get yet, but which they told him to sit tight for.

> *Outside comes the sound of carollers singing, "Joy to the World."*

He has to put somebody on the right path, you see. Now he's not a ghost, mind you. No, they don't like it when you call them that...

**TERESA**     Oh, listen. Listen. Carollers. Isn't that lovely?

> *DOUGLAS moves to the door. He opens it and shouts at the carollers.*

**DOUGLAS** Go away!!

> *The carollers stop. DOUGLAS closes the door, and moves back to ETHAN. TERESA looks out the window.*

Now, I've warned you about this, haven't I, Ethan? About this life after death, spirit world stuff?

**ETHAN**     But it's true.

**DOUGLAS** Shhhh! You didn't mention any of this to Miss Pike, did you?

**ETHAN**     Well, no, but...

**DOUGLAS** Good! You start talking like that around her and she'll be gone before you can say Ouija board. Now let's hear no more about it, all right?

**ETHAN**     But Douglas...

**DOUGLAS** Uh-uh-uh!! No more. Please. Now, how's that hot chocolate coming?

**ETHAN**     Just about ready.

**DOUGLAS** Good. Miss Pike, let me give you a hand there.

> *DOUGLAS moves to TERESA and begins decorating the tree.*
> *The door swings open and MARTIN enters. DOUGLAS moves*
> *to close the door.*

You didn't get that latch fixed like I told you, Ethan.

> *ETHAN has his back to the door as he fixes the hot chocolate.*

ETHAN      *(turning)* Hmm? *(He sees MARTIN.)* Martin.

DOUGLAS      What's that?

ETHAN      Uh... in the morning. I'll fix it in the morning.

> *DOUGLAS closes the door.*

DOUGLAS      There we go.

> *He returns to decorating the tree.*

MARTIN      Well, it's about time you three got back. How'd the egg thing go?

ETHAN      Good.

MARTIN      So you're all set now?

ETHAN      All set.

DOUGLAS      What was that?

ETHAN      I said all set. Are we all set for hot chocolate over there?

DOUGLAS      You bet we are. Bring it on.

MARTIN      Listen, Nancy, I just came to say goodbye. I have to go.

ETHAN      What?

MARTIN      I have to go. Time to move on.

ETHAN      What, you mean you're finished here?

MARTIN      Yeah.

ETHAN      But what about your assignment?

DOUGLAS      Ethan, who the heck are you talking to over there?

ETHAN      Uh... nobody.

MARTIN      Nobody?

ETHAN      Well, not nobody.

DOUGLAS      Well, who then?

MARTIN      Yeah, who then?

ETHAN      Myself. I was just talking to myself.

> *He takes the tray of hot chocolate to the living room area.*

**DOUGLAS** Well, you're makin' a fool out of yourself in front of this woman. She's going to think you're a flat out, certified...

*DOUGLAS freezes. TERESA freezes.*

**MARTIN** That's better. Nice fella, but awfully yappy, isn't he?

**ETHAN** What happened?

**MARTIN** I froze time.

**ETHAN** What?

**MARTIN** I froze time. I just learned it. Neat, huh?

**ETHAN** You mean, time is frozen everywhere?

**MARTIN** Everywhere.

**ETHAN** France?

**MARTIN** Frozen.

**ETHAN** China?

**MARTIN** Frozen.

**ETHAN** Mexico?

**MARTIN** Frozito.

**ETHAN** Wow. What about me? Why aren't I frozen?

**MARTIN** Because you're with me.

*He slaps ETHAN on the back.*

**ETHAN** Wait a minute. I felt that. You can touch me.

**MARTIN** That's right. That's what I said. You're with me now.

**ETHAN** But, you're dead.

**MARTIN** Oh, sure. Keep throwing that in my face.

**ETHAN** But I'm not dead, am I?

**MARTIN** No, no.

**ETHAN** So am I in the spirit world, or are you in the real world?

**MARTIN** Neither. We're on kind of a bridge that joins both worlds.

**ETHAN** A bridge?

**MARTIN** Yeah. Don't look down.

*ETHAN, startled, looks down.*

Listen, I've gotta run. *(moves right)*

**ETHAN** Wait? You can't stay a bit longer?

MARTIN    Stay? Why would I want to stay? No, I'm anxious to get to where I'm going. See what it's like there. I hope it's warm. *(looking up)* Well... not too warm.

ETHAN    But I thought it might be nice to spend a Christmas together.

MARTIN    No. No can do.

ETHAN    It's just one more day?

MARTIN    No. Besides, they're very strict. Once your assignment is completed, you've got to move on.

ETHAN    And you've completed yours?

MARTIN    Yeah.

ETHAN    What was it?

MARTIN    It was nothing. Not even worth talking about. So, anyway, that's it. Time to hit the road. It was nice seeing you again, brother.

ETHAN    Wait a minute. It was me, wasn't it? I was the assignment. I was the one you had to set on the right path.

MARTIN    No.

ETHAN    Sure it was. With the eggs and Teresa and all that.

MARTIN    No, it wasn't you, Ethan.

ETHAN    Well, who was it?

MARTIN    It was me. I was my assignment. I had to set myself on the right path.

ETHAN    I don't understand.

MARTIN    Ethan, I'm sorry. I took something from you a long time ago that I shouldn't have.

ETHAN    What?

MARTIN    *(beat)* Me. Your brother. And the love that you should've had from your brother. I wasn't there for you. I let you down, Ethan, and I'm sorry. I don't expect sixty thousand eggs to make it right, but I've never been as creative as you, and it was the best I could come up with. Now, I've got to go. They don't like it if you don't come when you're called.

*He moves towards the door.*

ETHAN    I'm never going to see you again?

MARTIN    No. But that's okay. You're going to be just fine without me.

ETHAN    You think so?

**MARTIN** *(looks at TERESA and DOUGLAS)* I know so. You know, Ethan, I learned something here this week. Dad was right. I guess I should've listened to him. Things might've been different between us.

> *The door swings open. MARTIN moves to it.*

**ETHAN** Martin?

> *MARTIN stops. ETHAN moves to him and gives him a hug. MARTIN is surprised, and after a moment, hugs him back.*

**MARTIN** Yeah, well, I gotta go. Have a nice Christmas, Nancy, and uh… can I tell you one more thing?

**ETHAN** What?

**MARTIN** That is the ugliest Christmas tree I have ever seen. *(beat)* Goodbye, Ethan.

**ETHAN** Goodbye, Martin.

> *MARTIN moves outside. Suddenly, the outside is brightly illuminated.*

**MARTIN** Oh, sure. Now with the light!

> *The door closes. When it does, time unfreezes.*

**DOUGLAS** Lunatic!

> *He realizes that Ethan isn't where he was standing when they started this conversation.*

What the…. How'd you do that?

**ETHAN** Do what?

**DOUGLAS** That. You were just… I was… and now you're…

**ETHAN** You must be tired, Douglas. Come over here and have some hot chocolate, and then you can go home to your wife.

**TERESA** What's this?

**ETHAN** What?

> *TERESA moves out. She is carrying a small, wrapped parcel.*

**TERESA** This. I found it under the tree, but I don't think it was there a minute ago. At least I didn't see it. Here, Ethan. Open it.

> *TERESA hands the package to ETHAN.*

**ETHAN** Why me?

**TERESA** Well, it's got your name on it.

**ETHAN** What?

**TERESA** Yeah. See?

*She hands the gift to ETHAN.*

ETHAN    Did Caroline send me a gift, Douglas?

DOUGLAS Well, if she did, she didn't mention it to me.

TERESA    Open it.

*ETHAN opens the gift. It is the painting of his mother.*

DOUGLAS Well, look at that.

TERESA    Who is it?

ETHAN    It's... a portrait of my mother.

TERESA    Well, who could've sent that?

ETHAN    I think I have an idea.

DOUGLAS Well you know in my house, we have a tradition. We always toast the opening of the first Christmas gift. In fact, in my house we toast the opening of every gift. So what do you say?

*He picks up his hot chocolate.*

Here's to the first gift of Christmas.

*They all raise their glasses.*

TERESA    And to good friends.

ETHAN    And to family.

*They toast. A light shines down on ETHAN. He holds his glass up to the heavens. Lights down.*

*End.*

# Dear Santa

*Dear Santa* was first produced at Theatre Orangeville, December 5 to 22, 2002, with the following cast and production team:

| | |
|---|---|
| SANTA CLAUS | John Dolan |
| ALGERNON GLADSTONE | Avery Saltzman |
| LOU FLAPDOODLE | Douglas Chamberlain |
| BOZIDAR | Stephen Guy-McGrath |
| KIT BISHOP | Siobhan O'Brien |
| OCTAVIA | Lezlie Wade |

**Elves**

| | |
|---|---|
| BALDERDASH | Katelyn Cassin |
| FIDDLESTICKS | Nancy Robinson |
| PIFFLE | Nicole Jedrzejko |
| YEEGADS/MICHAEL BISHOP | Dean Harris |
| SKIFFLE | Ariel Little-Alcorn |
| PHOOEY | Olivia Turley |
| SHORT STACK | Cheyanne Vandervoort |

Director: David Nairn
Set designer: Stephen Degenstein
Lighting designer: Simon Day
Stage manager: Laura-Lynn Reid

Original song: "This is My Christmas." Music by Steve Thomas, lyrics by Norm Foster.

**Characters**

| | |
|---|---|
| SANTA CLAUS | |
| ALGERNON GLADSTONE | Santa's Chief of Staff. |
| KIT BISHOP | A girl in her late teens. |
| BOZIDAR | Santa's foreman. He speaks with a Russian accent. |
| OCTAVIA | Santa's housekeeper. |
| LOU FLAPDOODLE | Sleigh salesman. |
| MICHAEL BISHOP | Kit's brother. |

Non-speaking parts: Mrs. Bishop, choir, assorted elves.

Note: The inhabitants of the North Pole are ageless, whether they have worked there for fifty-eight years or three hundred years.

# ACT ONE Scene One

*Time: The present.*

*Place: The North Pole. SANTA's office.*

*The play takes place in SANTA's office and the workshop. The office can be represented by just a desk and a chair. The workshop is a much bigger area with workbenches and toys. There should be two entrances stage left and two entrances stage right. When the scene is in the workshop, one entrance is from the laundry room, the sewing room, and OCTAVIA's room; one entrance is from outside. One entrance is from BOZIDAR's room and the elves quarters; one entrance is a back entrance. When the scene is in SANTA's office, one entrance is from outside, one entrance is from SANTA's living quarters, one entrance is a back entrance, and one is to another part of SANTA's house. Doors are not required. The entrances are merely from hallways.*

*As the lights come up, SANTA Claus and his chief of staff ALGERNON Gladstone enter the office. ALGERNON is carrying a large, elf-type cap. SANTA is wearing his "everyday" clothes—sweatpants and an old sweater. He also wears his SANTA hat.*

**AL**     Santa, please, I'm begging you, don't make me wear the hat.

**SANTA**     It's Christmastime, Algernon, and this is the North Pole. And when it's Christmastime at the North Pole, everybody wears the hat. It's part of the seasonal costume.

**AL**     No, I understand that. And on the elves I can see it. They look cute in the hats. They look downright elfish. But I'm your chief of staff. I'm supposed to command respect. How am I going to get any respect wearing the silly hat? Grown-up people who wear the hat look like buffoons.

**SANTA**     I wear the hat.

**AL**     And you look terrific in the hat. You are the hat. When people think of the hat, they think of you. But me, I put it on, I look like a garden gnome. I look like I should be standing watch over your petunias.

**SANTA**     Al, how long have you worked here?

**AL**     Fifty-eight years.

**SANTA**     And every year we have this same discussion.

**AL**     And isn't it getting just a little tiresome.

**SANTA**     It certainly is. Now, put the hat on.

**AL**     Santa...

**SANTA**    Al. Put on the hat.

**AL**    All right, you're the boss, but it's going to look silly.

    *AL puts the hat on. It is far too big and falls down over his face.*

Well, what do you think?

**SANTA**    Take if off. You look silly.

**AL**    Thank you.

    *He takes the hat off and sets it on SANTA's desk.*

You do that every year just to get a good laugh, don't you?

**SANTA**    Yes. And it cracks me up every time.

    *SANTA takes off his own hat and puts on a ball cap.*

All right, let's get down to business. What does my schedule look like today?

**AL**    *(reading from his notebook)* Well, it's a busy one, Santa. Right after breakfast you have a meeting with the sleigh salesman.

**SANTA**    Sleigh salesman?

**AL**    Yeah. I told you about this last week. He's got a new sleigh he wants you to try out.

**SANTA**    What's wrong with the sleigh I've got?

**AL**    Santa, come on. It was made during the Renaissance. It's five hundred years old.

**SANTA**    Oh, I think it's still got a lot of miles left in it.

**AL**    A lot of miles? Santa, you've driven that thing into the ground. Plus I don't think the sleigh or the reindeer are meeting today's emissions standards.

**SANTA**    Well, I think the sleigh is fine.

**AL**    Well, will you at least meet with the man? I mean, he's come all the way up here from Detroit.

**SANTA**    All right then, if he's come all this way, I'll meet with him as a courtesy.

**AL**    Thank you. Then at ten o'clock you're going to listen to the choir to hear how they're doing.

**SANTA**    And how are they doing?

**AL**    Well, word on the street isn't good, Santa. Ever since the choir master retired they've been rehearsing on their own and... well, I understand the rest of the staff has taken to wearing earmuffs whenever they pass the rehearsal hall.

**SANTA**    Well, of course they're wearing earmuffs. It's cold outside.

AL        Yeah. I'm sure that's the reason. Now, at ten-thirty it's your morning snack, at eleven o'clock it's brunch, and at twelve o'clock it's lunch. And then from twelve-thirty to one I've scheduled some indigestion. At two o'clock you're parachuting into the West Edmonton Mall. That'll be at the south entrance. And please be careful this time. You remember last year you misjudged your approach and landed on that sausage vendor's cart.

SANTA     I didn't misjudge my approach. I was hungry.

AL        Well, this year just land where they ask you to and we'll order in some ribs. And then at three-thirty you have a meeting in Paris with the Belanger twins.

SANTA     Jacques and Maurice.

AL        Yes. They want to talk to you about the lumps of coal you left in their stockings last Christmas. Apparently they've been very good this year and they want to make sure you're aware of that.

SANTA     Oh, I know they've been good. I've been watching and I've been very impressed.

AL        Yeah, well, personally I think you should give them the coal again this year, just to make sure they get the message.

SANTA     Well, that's why I'm Santa Claus and you're not. What's next?

AL        All right, let's see here. From Paris you go to Thailand…

SANTA     Oh, I love Thai food.

AL        Uh-huh. And then to Switzerland…

SANTA     Mmmmm, schnitzel.

AL        Yeah. And then it's back here to spend some time in the workshop.

SANTA     Well, that sounds like another full day.

*The phone rings. AL picks it up.*

AL        Santa's office. Al Gladstone here…. You'd like to speak to Santa Claus? Yeah, you and a billion others like you…. Well, I'm sorry but Santa's in a meeting right now.

SANTA     Al?

AL        No, he really can't be disturbed. I'm sorry…. That's right…. Well, I'll tell him you called, but I wouldn't count on him getting back to you anytime soon. Okay. Bye-bye.

*AL hangs up the telephone.*

Call your wife when you get a chance. *(looking over his notes)* Now, what else have we got here? Oh! I spoke with the Tooth Fairy yesterday. She was trying to set up a speaking tour for the two of you for next summer in South America. But here's the funny part. She wants top billing. Yeah, she wants to call it the "Tooth Fairy and Santa Claus Get Silly in Chile Tour." So I said to her, I said, "Tooth, come on. You visit maybe eight million people in a year. Santa does the whole world in one night. No way you should get top billing." So anyway, she's going to think about it and have her people get back to me. Yeah, like the Tooth Fairy needs people.

SANTA Well, you look after that for me, Al. That's why I hired you.

AL No problem. Oh, listen, can I ask you a tiny favour, Santa?

SANTA Certainly, what is it?

AL Can I hitch a ride with you on Christmas Eve? I need a lift to the Cayman Islands. That's where I'm spending Christmas this year.

SANTA Oh. All right. Are you spending it with friends, relatives?

AL No, just me.

SANTA Al, you're not spending Christmas alone again, are you?

AL Hey, I've done it every other year. Why should this year be any different?

SANTA Why? Because Christmas is a time to be shared with loved ones, that's why.

AL Yeah, well I don't have any loved ones, Santa, and you know what? I like it that way. I'd much rather relax on a beach on Christmas morning than spend my time opening presents that people felt they had to buy for me.

SANTA Algernon, that is entirely the wrong attitude to take towards Christmas. Christmas is a time of joy and if I were you, I would appreciate Christmas for the way it brings people together. For the way it makes each one of us feel towards one another.

AL Well, that's why I'm Al Gladstone and you're not.

    *BOZIDAR enters from outside.*

BOZIDAR Santa Claus? Excuse me for interrupting, but I need to be beating your eardrum.

SANTA What was that?

AL He wants to talk to you.

SANTA Oh, certainly, Bozidar. Come right in. What can I do for you?

BOZIDAR Well... *(He sees the hat.)* Oh, did you pull hat gag on Al again?

SANTA Yes.

BOZIDAR And it works?

SANTA Like a charm.

BOZIDAR I love that bit.

*SANTA and BOZIDAR laugh.*

**SANTA**    It is a good one, isn't it?

**BOZIDAR**    I'm sorry I miss it.

**AL**    Yeah, okay, get on with your business, Bozidar. Santa and I have a schedule to keep.

**BOZIDAR**    Oh, right. Well, Santa, I am bringing good news. The North Pole Special just pulled in with rest of toy-making supplies.

**SANTA**    Oh, that is good news. Excellent news!

**BOZIDAR**    I know. I was so happy I had to pinch my elf to make sure I wasn't dreaming.

**SANTA**    Well, you see that the supplies get over to the workshop as quickly as possible, Bozidar. And make sure they shipped everything we asked for. All the wood, the wood glue, the nuts and bolts, the dolls' eyes, everything.

**BOZIDAR**    You got it. I will check, double-check, and bodycheck.

**AL**    Hey, there should be a case of scones there too. See that it's sent to my cabin, will you?

**BOZIDAR**    Okey donkey. What is scones?

**AL**    Well, it's like a big biscuit and they go great with a cup of tea.

**SANTA**    All right, Bozidar, just go please.

**BOZIDAR**    That's for sure. I am gone before you can say "Hit the road, Jack Frost."

*BOZIDAR exists to outside.*

**SANTA**    All right, let's head off to breakfast, shall we? We'll stop at the workshop on the way and let the elves know that the supplies are in.

**AL**    Oh, no. You want me to go to the workshop with you?

**SANTA**    What's wrong with the workshop?

**AL**    Oh, it's those elves. I mean, they're so cheerful all the time. And they're always singing, and they whistle while they work.

**SANTA**    That's the seven dwarfs.

**AL**    Elves, dwarfs.

**SANTA**    You're coming with me, Al. I think you could use a little cheerfulness.

*AL picks up the hat.*

Oh, no. Leave the hat. I'll need it again next year.

> *SANTA laughs. AL puts the hat on SANTA's desk and they exit to outside. Lights down. Music up. An up-tempo pop or rock song of the day.*

## ACT ONE Scene Two

> *Time: A few minutes later.*
>
> *Place: SANTA's workshop.*
>
> *Lights up on the workshop. SANTA's elves are working and bopping to the music. SKIFFLE stands watch near a window.*

**SKIFFLE**  He's coming! He's coming!

> *SKIFFLE throws some pixie dust at the radio and the music stops. All of the elves begin to sing a Christmas song.*
>
> *SANTA and ALGERNON enter.*

**AL**  Oh, I knew it.

> *The ELVES continue to sing another verse.*

**SANTA**  *(applauding)* Very nice. Very nice.

**SKIFFLE**  Oh, Santa, you surprised us.

**ELVES**  Good morning, Santa Claus!

**SANTA**  Good morning, my elves.

**ELVES**  Good morning, Mr. Gallstone!

**AL**  It's Gladstone! *(to SANTA)* They're doing that on purpose you know. They're making fun of me.

**SANTA**  Oh, piffle.

**PIFFLE**  Yes, Santa?

**SANTA**  Oh, no, I wasn't talking to you, Piffle. I was just... never mind. Al, the elves would never make fun of you.

**SKIFFLE**  Did you get him with the hat gag yet, Santa?

**SANTA**  Oh, yes. You should have been there.

> *SANTA and the ELVES laugh.*

**AL**  All right, all right, quiet down! Santa's got some news for you. *(to the shortest elf)* That goes for you too, Short Stack. Pay attention.

**SANTA**  Well, the news is good this morning, everyone. The North Pole Special has just arrived with our supplies.

> *The ELVES cheer.*

And that means that we'll be able to make the Christmas Eve deadline again this year.

*The ELVES cheer.*

**AL**        Santa, you always make the deadline. When have you never made the deadline?

**SANTA**        Well, nineteen forty-seven was close. We had a blackout that year. Couldn't see a thing in here. Oh, what a mess that was. Dolls were going out with three noses. We had toy soldiers wearing evening gowns. It was a fiasco.

*OCTAVIA enters the workshop carrying a laundry basket.*

**OCTAVIA**    All right, this is it. I am not going to tell you elves again. The laundry hamper is not a basketball hoop. No more jump shots with your underwear. Your bathroom is littered with elf shorts.

**SANTA**        Good morning, Octavia.

**OCTAVIA**    Oh, good morning, Santa Claus. Good morning, Algernon.

**AL**        Octavia.

**SANTA**        Oh Octavia, when you get a moment I've got a hole in the elbow of my other suit that needs to be sewn up, and my Christmas Eve pants need to be pressed as well.

**OCTAVIA**    Oh, Santa, come on, what am I, your housekeeper?

**SANTA**        …Yes, you are.

**OCTAVIA**    Oh, right. I am. Okay, I'll get right on it.

**SANTA**        Thank you. Now, let's see how our work is progressing here. *(moving to one of the elves at a workbench)* Oh, this is very nice. Very nice indeed.

*OCTAVIA moves to ALGERNON.*

**OCTAVIA**    How are you this morning, Algernon?

**AL**        Oh, I'm good. You know, busy.

**OCTAVIA**    Uh-huh.

**AL**        But that's the way I like it, you know? Gotta keep busy. Otherwise, what is there to do up here? I mean, how many times can you play flashlight tag with Rudolph?

**OCTAVIA**    Right.

**AL**        And how are you doing?

**OCTAVIA**    Oh, I'm busy too. Being the North Pole housekeeper is almost like having a full-time job.

**AL**        It is your full-time job.

**OCTAVIA**   Oh, right. So, are you coming to the wrap party on Christmas Eve?

**AL**   The wrap party?

**OCTAVIA**   Yeah, you know, when we wrap all the gifts?

**AL**   Oh the wrap party. Yes. Well, I'm going to have a million things to do on Christmas Eve, Octavia. I've got to pack and everything, so...

**OCTAVIA**   Oh, are you going away again this year?

**AL**   Yeah. Yeah.

**OCTAVIA**   Heading down south?

**AL**   Well I would have to, wouldn't I?

**OCTAVIA**   I beg your pardon?

**AL**   This is the North Pole. South is the only direction from here.

**OCTAVIA**   Oh, so it is. You'd think I'd know that by now, but no. So, you won't be coming to the party then?

**AL**   No, I don't think so.

**OCTAVIA**   Oh, that's too bad.

**AL**   Why?

**OCTAVIA**   Oh, no reason. It's just that you're one of the few people up here that I can talk to face to face.

**AL**   Oh, I see.

**OCTAVIA**   I talk to the elves for too long and I'm hunched over for a week. Well, I'd better get over to Santa's office and pick up that suit and those pants.

**AL**   Yeah, sure.

**OCTAVIA**   Maybe I'll see you at breakfast.

**AL**   Maybe.

**OCTAVIA**   Oh, and just a word of warning. Watch out for that hat gag. I think Santa's going to pull it on you again this year.

**AL**   I'll be ready.

   *OCTAVIA exits out the rear. As she is leaving, BOZIDAR enters from the outside.*

**BOZIDAR**   Morning, Octavia.

**OCTAVIA**   Morning, Bozidar.

   *OCTAVIA exits.*

**BOZIDAR**   Santa?

SANTA        Yes, Bozidar?

BOZIDAR     Santa, we've got problem at train station.

SANTA        Problem? What kind of problem? Did they forget the supplies?

BOZIDAR     Uh… well… no. Supplies are fine. Supplies are in good supply. You don't have to worrywart about that.

SANTA        Well, what's the problem then?

BOZIDAR     Well, now is not big problem. It is nothing to get your blouse in a sheepshank about.

SANTA        My what?

AL           Your shirt in a knot.

SANTA        Oh.

BOZIDAR     Right. Is smaller problem. Well, not real small. Is somewhere between small and big. Smig, I guess.

SANTA        Bozidar, get to the point please.

BOZIDAR     Well, I can explain to you better in your office. Can you meet me there in time it takes to prepare minute-rice?

SANTA        I beg your pardon?

AL           Five minutes.

SANTA        Oh, of course. Certainly. We'll be right over.

BOZIDAR     Good. I see you there in two shakes of a Lamborghini.

            *BOZIDAR exits out the rear entrance.*

SANTA        All right, Al, let's go. *(to the ELVES)* Now, don't forget to stop for breakfast everyone. It's the most important meal of the day, you know.

ELVES        We will, Santa.

SANTA        *(to the ELVES)* Goodbye now.

ELVES        Goodbye, Santa! Goodbye, Mr. Flintstone!

AL           It's Gladstone!

            *AL exits. SANTA begins to exit, then stops and turns the radio back on. We hear the up-tempo music again. SANTA exits. The ELVES begin working and bopping.*

## ACT ONE Scene Three

> *Time: Five minutes later.*
>
> *Place: SANTA's office.*
>
> *As the lights come up, SANTA and AL enter the office.*

**AL**   No, I don't go in for those resort-type places. I mean, that's not roughing it. I want to get back to the land when I'm on vacation. Back to basics. No, this is a little grass hut right on the beach. No television, no phone, no bathroom.

**SANTA**  No bathroom?

**AL**   Nope.

**SANTA**  Well, what do you do when you need a bathroom?

**AL**   Oh, there's a resort right next door. I use theirs. And sometimes I go there if there's something on TV that I want to watch.

**SANTA**  Or if you need to use the phone?

**AL**   Yeah.

> *OCTAVIA enters from SANTA's living quarters. She is carrying a pair of SANTA's pants.*

**OCTAVIA** Santa?

**SANTA**  Yes, Octavia?

**OCTAVIA** Oh, hello again, Algernon.

**AL**   Yeah, hi.

**OCTAVIA** Are these the pants you wanted ironed, Santa?

**SANTA**  Yes, those are the ones.

**OCTAVIA** Fine. Oh, and can I make a suggestion? I don't think red is your colour. It's not a slimming tone, if you know what I'm saying. If I were you I'd be looking at blacks and navies.

**SANTA**  Santa Claus wearing black? I don't know about that, Octavia

**OCTAVIA** Why not? I mean, it's not like you're known for your red suit.

**AL**   Actually, he is known for his red suit.

**OCTAVIA** Oh. *(to SANTA)* Forget I mentioned it. *(to ALGERNON)* So, we meet again.

**AL**   Yeah, so we do.

**OCTAVIA** Strange, huh? Sometimes I don't see you for days, and this morning I see you twice in a matter of minutes. Do you think its fate, or is it just destiny?

**AL**   Fate is destiny.

**OCTAVIA**   It is? Well, shut my mouth.

> *BOZIDAR enters with KIT Bishop. He is pulling her by the arm.*

**KIT**   Hey, let go of me, you big goon. Let go!

**BOZIDAR**   This is the problem I was telling you about. She is a stone's throw away.

**SANTA**   A what?

**BOZIDAR**   A stone's throw away.

**SANTA**   I'm sorry. A what?

**AL**   A stowaway.

**SANTA**   Oh.

**BOZIDAR**   Yes. She was on North Pole Special. She was hiding in Boxcar Willie.

**SANTA**   Well now, young lady. The North Pole Special is not a passenger train. It's for supplies only. What's your name?

**KIT**   Kit. What's yours?

**AL**   Hey, don't be a wisenheimer.

**SANTA**   Never mind, Al. I can handle this. I'm Santa Claus, Kit. And this is Octavia, Bozidar, and Algernon.

**KIT**   What is this, the North Pole or the land of stupid names?

**BOZIDAR**   Well, isn't that the pot calling the kettle of fish?

**SANTA**   All right, Bozidar, Octavia, you two can go on about your work, please.

**BOZIDAR**   Are you sure, Santa? Are you sure you'll be all right here with this one?

**SANTA**   Oh I think I'll be fine, Bozidar, don't worry.

**BOZIDAR**   All right, but if she is giving you any trouble, you just call my name and I'll be coming in a hurry. You no having to worry. 'Cause baby ain't no mountain peaking high enough.

> *BOZIDAR exits outside. OCTAVIA exits to SANTA's living quarters.*

**SANTA**   So, which Kit are you?

**KIT**   What do you mean, which Kit?

**SANTA**   Well, I have a lot of Kits on my list. Thousands in fact.

| | |
|---|---|
| **KIT** | I'm Kit Bishop. |
| **SANTA** | The Boston Kit Bishop, or the Windsor Kit Bishop? |
| **KIT** | Windsor. |
| **SANTA** | All right, now we're getting somewhere. And tell me Kit Bishop, why did you travel all the way up here to the North Pole? |
| **KIT** | I had to bring you something. |

*She takes an envelope out of her coat and hands it to SANTA.*

| | |
|---|---|
| **SANTA** | What's this? A letter? |
| **KIT** | No, it's a ceiling fan. What does it look like? |
| **AL** | Hey, Orphan Annie, save the attitude for your schoolteachers. This is Santa Claus you're talking to here. |
| **SANTA** | It's all right, Al. It's all right. *(to KIT)* So, you came all the way up here to deliver a letter, did you? |
| **KIT** | Yeah. |
| **SANTA** | I see. Are you sure it wasn't because of that quarrel you had with your mother last week? |
| **KIT** | What quarrel? |
| **SANTA** | Oh come now, Kit. According to my sources, your mother scolded you last week because you did poorly on your history exam at school. And you said you did poorly because you had too much work to do at home and you didn't have time to study. Now was that you, or was that the Boston Kit Bishop? |
| **KIT** | All right it was me. But I didn't come up here because of that. I just came to deliver the letter. |
| **SANTA** | Fine. And what's in the letter? |
| **KIT** | I don't know. I didn't write it. It's from my little brother. |
| **SANTA** | Michael? |
| **KIT** | Right. He says he sent you a letter last year, but he doesn't think you got it because you didn't give him what he asked for. So this year he asked me to hand deliver one to you. |
| **SANTA** | And you did all this, sneaking onto a train, riding for days in a cold boxcar, probably going hungry too, all for your little brother. |
| **KIT** | Naw, I didn't go hungry. I found a case of scones on the train. |
| **AL** | Oh, come on! |
| **SANTA** | Nevertheless, you did all of this for Michael. |
| **KIT** | Well, sure I did. He's a good kid. I do whatever I can for him. |

SANTA     I know you do.

KIT       Yeah, and it would be nice if you did too.

SANTA     Pardon me?

KIT       Don't let him down again like you did last year. Make sure he gets what he wants this time.

AL        Okay, sister, that's it. Hit the road.

          *AL takes KIT by the arm.*

SANTA     Al, no.

AL        Santa, we can't have street urchins coming in here and making demands like that.

KIT       I'm not a street urchin!

AL        Yeah, tell it to the Easter Bunny.

SANTA     Al, wait. Before you go throwing Miss Bishop into the snow, let me tell you a bit about her.

AL        Then can I throw her out?

SANTA     If, when I've finished, you still feel that she deserves to be thrown out, then by all means, you may.

AL        Good enough. Lay it on me.

SANTA     Well, her father passed away when Kit was only nine years old. Her mother works twelve hours a day making pottery and other craftwork, which she sells at the local market to make ends meet. Kit goes to school during the day and works a few nights a week at a clothing store. Of course, the money she makes goes right into the family account to help her mother pay the bills. At home, Kit cooks all of the meals and does the lion's share of the housework. Unfortunately, all of this leaves her very little time to pursue her first love, which is music. Kit would like to be a professional singer and a songwriter someday but the way things are going right now, she may have to put her dreams on hold so that she can help see her family through these difficult times. And there you have it. That is the story of our young Kit Bishop.

          *AL looks at KIT for a second.*

AL        Okay, out you go!

SANTA     Al!

AL        What?

SANTA     That story didn't touch you at all?

AL        Touch me? Are you kidding? Compared to my childhood, it was the feel-good story of the year!

SANTA     You'll have to excuse Al, Miss Bishop. I'm afraid all these years as my chief of staff have left him a little too businesslike. Now, let's just see what your brother has to say in this letter.

> SANTA opens the letter and begins to read to himself. As he does this, AL and KIT begin a war of words under their breath.

KIT     You couldn't throw me out, Gomer.

AL     Oh I could throw you out all right, powder puff.

KIT     Yeah, you and what elf army?

AL     I wouldn't need an army. I could toss you like a Greek salad.

KIT     Oh yeah?

AL     Yeah.

KIT     Well, I could drop you like a sack of toys.

AL     Oh, you are so lucky you're a girl.

KIT     You got that right!

SANTA     (folding the letter up) Hmm-hmm. All right then.

KIT     Yeah, okay, fine. Well, you got the letter so I'll be going now.

SANTA     Going where?

KIT     Home.

SANTA     And how do you propose to do that?

KIT     On the train, of course.

SANTA     Oh, I'm afraid that won't be possible.

KIT     Oh, what, you're not going to let me ride the train back?

SANTA     The train's not going back.

KIT     It's what?

SANTA     It's a supply train and it's just delivered our last shipment of supplies. It won't be going back until production begins again in March.

KIT     March?!

AL     Nice planning, Einstein.

KIT     So how am I supposed to get back home? I have to be home for Christmas.

SANTA     Oh, I'm sure we'll figure something out. In the meantime, maybe you'd like to join us for breakfast. And then after breakfast I'll get Al to show you around.

AL     Oh, Santa, don't make me play nursemaid to her.

KIT      *(to AL)* Hey, I can take care of myself. Don't you worry about that.

AL      Oh, like I'm gonna worry about you.

SANTA      All right now, that's enough out of both of you. Al, you'll show Kit around while I meet with the sleigh salesman. Now let's get some food before I waste away to nothing.

> *SANTA exits outside.*

KIT      That could take a while.

AL      Just get going, would you.

KIT      Hey don't rush me, Wilbur.

AL      Oh, I'll rush you all right.

KIT      Oh, I don't think so.

AL      Oh, I'll rush you all right.

KIT      Oh, I don't think so.

AL      Well think again, Artful Dodger.

> *AL and KIT exit outside. OCTAVIA enters from SANTA's living quarters carrying SANTA's coat. She picks up SANTA's pants. As she is walking by his desk, she notices the letter. She picks it up and starts reading. Over, we hear the voice of MICHAEL reading the letter.*

MICHAEL      Dear Santa, I hope I have been a good boy this year, because I am asking you for something that is very important. Could you please bring my sister Kit some Christmas spirit. She doesn't seem to have as much fun at Christmas as she used to, and it makes me sad to see her unhappy. Thank you, Santa. I love you. Michael Bishop.

> *OCTAVIA sets the letter down and exits outside. Lights down.*

## ACT ONE Scene Four

> *Time: About an hour later.*
>
> *Place: The workshop.*
>
> *The lights come up to reveal an empty workshop. AL and KIT enter.*

AL      Oh, good. The elves aren't back from breakfast yet. Let's make this quick before they show up. Now this is the workshop. This is where all of the toys are made. We start production around March and we work continuously, day and night, until Christmas Eve.

KIT      Day and night? Don't the elves get tired?

AL          Don't worry. We have three shifts of elves who work eight hours each. Do you think Santa Claus is going to overwork his elves? How would that look in the press? Plus, they get some nice fringe benefits. There's plenty of good skiing in the area, they get into all the movies at children's prices, and they get a day off to celebrate Mickey Rooney's birthday. *(pointing off, right)* Now back through there is the laundry room, and the sewing room, and Octavia's quarters. *(pointing off, left)* And through there, that's the elves' quarters and Bozidar's room.

KIT         So, what did you mean back there about your childhood?

AL          What?

KIT         Your childhood. You implied that it was rough.

AL          So what if it was?

KIT         Nothing. I was just wondering if it was as rough as mine.

AL          What? Hey, ground control to Major Kit! Being a kid isn't easy at the best of times. Every kid has it rough, and every one for different reasons. You grew up without a father. I grew up without a mother. So what? There are kids who have both parents and still have a rough go of it. Some of them lack confidence. Some have trouble making friends. Some can't play sports as good as the others. Some have trouble with schoolwork or think they look funny in their glasses or don't know how to swim or can't ride a bike and on and on and on. To the rest of us, these seem like small problems, but when it's our problem, it's the biggest problem in the world. And sometimes you think you'll never overcome it. But, we always do. So put your violin back in the case because I can't hear it.

KIT         What happened to you mother?

AL          She got sick and she never recovered.

KIT         Oh.

AL          So, my dad raised me. He did a good job too. Taught me how to be strong. How to survive in the business world.

KIT         I miss my dad. Especially around Christmas.

AL          Yeah, well my dad wasn't big on the whole Christmas thing. He was a truck driver and to him Christmas was just downtime. A time when he didn't make much money.

          *OCTAVIA enters from the sewing area carrying SANTA's coat.*

OCTAVIA   Oh, hello, Algernon.

AL          Octavia.

OCTAVIA   Do you believe this? Three times in one morning.

AL          What?

OCTAVIA   You and me. Running into one another. This is the third time this morning.

AL   Really? I've seen you twice already this morning?

OCTAVIA   Yes, silly. First here, and then a few minutes ago in Santa's office.

AL   Oh, right. Right.

OCTAVIA   We must be setting some kind of record or something.

AL   Yes, we'll have to get Guinness on the phone.

OCTAVIA   Who?

AL   Guinness. The people who publish the book of world records.

OCTAVIA   There's a book of world records?

AL   Yes.

OCTAVIA   What's it called?

AL   *The Guinness Book of World Records.*

OCTAVIA   Well, string my beans. Well, I'd better get Santa's coat back to him. Maybe I'll run into you later on. Well, probably not. I mean, that would be four times in one day. That really would be a record, wouldn't it?

AL   Yes, I guess it would.

OCTAVIA   Well, goodbye.

AL   Yeah, bye.

> *OCTAVIA exits out the back way.*

> *(to KIT)* Okay, let's go.

KIT   She likes you.

AL   What?

KIT   She likes you.

AL   What?

KIT   That woman. She likes you. She's got a crush on you.

AL   A crush? Octavia? She does not.

KIT   She does. I can tell.

AL   You cannot. How can you tell?

KIT   She gets all flustered around you. And she makes small talk so she can be around you for an extra few seconds. No, she's definitely got a crush on you.

AL   Oh, I don't believe that.

> *OCTAVIA enters again.*

**OCTAVIA**    Oh. Algernon?

**AL**    Yes?

**OCTAVIA**    I was just wondering. Did you see the weather forecast for tonight?

**AL**    Weather forecast? No, I didn't.

**OCTAVIA**    Well, apparently it's going down to minus fifty-five.

**AL**    Minus fifty-five. Wow, a heat wave. I'll have to take that extra blanket off my bed.

**OCTAVIA**    *(She laughs.)* Oh, Algernon. You're so funny.

    *OCTAVIA exits.*

**KIT**    Oh man, you didn't see that?

**AL**    See what?

**KIT**    Making small talk about the weather. Laughing at your dumb joke. Oh, she's got it bad.

**AL**    Ah, you don't know what you're talking about. And it wasn't a dumb joke.

**KIT**    Oh, it was dumb all right.

    *Off, we hear the ELVES singing a rather odd choice of music. The song could be anything from "Oklahoma" to "Penny Lane" to "El Paso." Anything that seems out of place.*

**AL**    Oh no. They're coming. Come on. Out the back door.

    *AL and KIT move towards the back exit. Just as they get to the exit, a group of ELVES enter singing. AL grabs KIT and pulls her towards the front door.*

No, come on! Out this way!

    *Just as AL and KIT get to the front door, another group of ELVES enter singing.*

All right, all right! Hold it down, would you?!

    *The ELVES stop singing.*

Thank you.

**ELVES**    You're welcome, Mr. Rhinestone.

**AL**    Gladstone! *(to KIT)* All right, as long as they're here I might as well introduce you. These are the elves. You saw them at breakfast. They were the ones eating shortbread. *(to the ELVES)* Elves, this is Kit Bishop.

**KIT**    Hi.

**ELVES**    Good morning, Kit Bishop!

AL          Sure, you get her name right.

          *BOZIDAR enters from outside.*

BOZIDAR  Oh, there you are, Al. I have been looking for you high and Lois Lane.

AL          Well, you found me, Bozidar. What is it?

BOZIDAR  Well, I have bad news about scones.

AL          Uh-huh.

BOZIDAR  They are all gone. Disappeared. They vanish into thinning hair.

AL          Thin air.

BOZIDAR  What?

AL          It's thin air.

BOZIDAR  Oh. Must be the altitude.

AL          Right. Well, thanks for telling me, Bozidar.

BOZIDAR  You are welcome.

          *BOZIDAR doesn't move.*

AL          All right, you can go.

          *BOZIDAR stands there, looking nervous.*

    What's the matter?

BOZIDAR  Well, I got confession to make.

AL          Confession about what?

BOZIDAR  Well, I not tell Santa Claus whole truth and nothing but the truth about supplies.

AL          You didn't?

BOZIDAR  Well, I not want to worry him. He already got too much playing gentle on his mind. I shouldn't even tell you. In fact, I won't. Just forget I threw it up.

AL          Bozidar?

BOZIDAR  No. I never tell. A team of wild horseflies couldn't drag it out of me.

AL          Bozidar, please?

BOZIDAR  All right, if you are going to get nasty, I talk. The thing is, we not get all of our supplies like I tell Santa we did.

AL          What do you mean? What didn't we get?

BOZIDAR  Well, hold on to your hat size. We not get any wood glue.

*The ELVES gasp.*

AL       What?!

BOZIDAR    Not a drop. We order two hundred gallons wood glue, we get butkus.

AL       Oh no. This is terrible.

BOZIDAR    It is apostrophe.

AL       Catastrophe.

BOZIDAR    Is that too.

AL       My goodness, we've got rocking horses to glue together. Marionettes, hockey sticks, guitars.

BOZIDAR    Desks, doll houses, toy boats.

AL       Fire trucks, carousels, scooters.

KIT      Can I make a suggestion?

AL       Excuse me? Do you mind? We're in the middle of a panic attack here.

KIT      But, it's not that difficult to—

AL       Uh-uh-uh-uh. Just let me think, would you, please? All right, Bozidar, you did the right thing by not telling Santa. He's got enough to worry about. Now what we have to do is come up with a glue substitute.

KIT      You can make your own glue.

AL       Look, I'm not going to tell you again. If I want your opinion.... What? Make our own glue?

KIT      Sure. My mother does it all the time for her crafts.

AL       How? How do you make glue? What do we need?

KIT      Well, you need non-fat milk, vinegar, baking soda, hot tap water, and some coffee filters.

AL       That's it? That's all we need?

KIT      That's it.

AL       And we can make glue from this?

KIT      You sure can.

BOZIDAR    Well, I'll be my uncle's monkey.

AL       All right, that's what we'll do then. We'll make our own glue. Can you show us how?

KIT      What's in it for me?

AL       What?

KIT       What's in it for me if I help you?

AL         Oh, well, that's a charming attitude. I'm giving you a chance to save Christmas for children all over the world and all you can say is "what's in it for me?"

        *Beat. KIT doesn't answer.*

Ten bucks.

KIT       Done.

AL         Bozidar, loan me ten dollars.

BOZIDAR  What?!

AL         Loan me ten dollars till payday. You'll get it back.

BOZIDAR  *(taking out ten dollars)* Oh, sure I get it back. Famous last words. I still waiting for ten dollars you owe me from Stanley Cup bet.

AL         Hey, that goal was offside. No way I'm paying for that.

BOZIDAR  Well, then that makes you a Welshman.

        *BOZIDAR hands AL the money.*

AL         It's welcher. Thank you. *(giving the money to KIT)* There. Now let's go.

BOZIDAR  Wait a minute. Wait a minute. I don't mean to play devil's avocado, but how are we going to make glue without Santa Claus knowing?

AL         Hmm. That's right. We need to make it someplace where he won't find it. Ah! We'll make it in your room.

BOZIDAR  My room?

AL         Sure, it's perfect. It's close to the workshop and Santa never goes in there.

BOZIDAR  All right, but if Santa finds it, and is asking how it got there, I am saying I am clueless.

AL         Good. He'll believe that. Now, let's go over to the cafeteria and get all the supplies. *(to KIT)* And while we load up you can write out the formula for us. Let's ride!

        *BOZIDAR and KIT exit out the front way. Just as AL is about to leave, the ELVES speak in unison.*

ELVES    Goodbye, Mr. Tombstone.

AL         Hey! You're this close to becoming a charm bracelet, okay?

        *AL exits. The ELVES break into gales of laughter, slapping their knees, banging their desks, etc. Lights down.*

## ACT ONE Scene Five

*Time: Moments later.*

*Place: SANTA's office.*

*Lights come up to reveal SANTA sitting at his desk, looking at the letter. OCTAVIA enters from SANTA's living quarters.*

**OCTAVIA**   I hung your coat in your closet, Santa Claus, and your pants are ironed too.

**SANTA**   Thank you, Octavia. Thank you.

**OCTAVIA**   Anything wrong, Santa?

**SANTA**   Hmm?

**OCTAVIA**   You seem troubled. Is something wrong?

**SANTA**   Oh, no, no. It's just that some children's Christmas lists are harder to fill than others. There are some gifts that you can't put under a tree.

**OCTAVIA**   Oh, I'm sure you'll be able to do it. You always manage somehow.

**SANTA**   Well, I hope so. I certainly hope so. Oh, that reminds me. I haven't seen your Christmas list yet.

**OCTAVIA**   Oh I don't want anything, Santa. I'm fine.

**SANTA**   Are you sure?

**OCTAVIA**   Oh yeah.

**SANTA**   Oh come now, Octavia. There must be something I can get for you.

**OCTAVIA**   No. Unless you can open a person's eyes.

**SANTA**   What's that supposed to mean?

**OCTAVIA**   Well, there's a certain someone who I kind of like, but he doesn't seem to know I'm alive. I just think it would be nice if he noticed me, that's all. But, that's not the kind of request you handle, is it?

**SANTA**   Well, that does sound more like a job for my friend Cupid.

**OCTAVIA**   Yeah, and you don't want to step on his toes, what with him being armed and all. Well, don't worry about me this year, Santa. I'm sure you have more important cases to look after anyway.

**SANTA**   They're all important, Octavia. Each and every one. That's what makes my job so difficult.

**OCTAVIA**   Yeah. Well, I'd better get back to work. I don't want to fall behind. I mean, it's not like there's twenty-four hours in a day to do all this stuff.

SANTA   Yes. Have a nice day, Octavia.

> *OCTAVIA exits outside. SANTA looks at the letter again. After a moment there is a knock on the door.*

Come in.

> *LOU Flapdoodle enters from the outside.*

LOU   Santa Claus?

SANTA   Yes.

LOU   Well, of course you're Santa Claus. You're sitting there, you've got the beard, the belly. Who you gonna be? Pippi Longstocking? Come on. Santa, nice to meet you. The name is Louis Flapdoodle. I'm from the National Sleigh Company.

> *He moves to SANTA and shakes his hand.*

Your buddy, Al, said I should be here at nine-thirty sharp. I'm not late am I? Because my watch says nine-thirty on the nose. Look at that.

> *He shows SANTA his watch.*

It's a Rudolph the Red-Nosed Reindeer watch. So when I say it's nine-thirty on the nose, I mean it! Anyway, thank you for seeing me this morning, Santa. Can I call you Santa? What do you like? Santa, Kris, Nick, Père Noël? Last guy I knew who used that many names was on the run from John Law, but that's another story. So, what'll it be? Santa?

SANTA   Santa will do just fine.

LOU   Santa it is then. And you can call me Lou. Most folks call me Lucky Lou because I've had an uncommon run of good fortune where sleigh sales are concerned. I don't know what it is, but I always manage to close the deal. And they're honest deals too, Santa. Yes sir. I'm not a swindler. I'm not a charlatan. I'm not a fraud. Well, you know that. You're the guy who knows if we've been naughty or nice, right? You've seen my work. Besides, do you think I'm going to try and cheat Santa Claus? Not on your life. Mama Flapdoodle didn't raise no fool. I mean, trying to pull the wool over your eyes would be like trying to sneak a Butterball turkey past you. It ain't gonna happen, babe! Do you mind if I take my coat off, Santa, because I work better when I'm unrestricted. Would that be copacetic?

SANTA   Of course.

LOU   Thank you. Thank you very much. *(He takes his coat off.)* There we go. That's better. Cold up here. Well, it's the North Pole. What's it gonna be? Beach weather? Of course not. You know what it's gonna be? It's gonna be sleigh weather. That's what it's gonna be. And that's why I'm here, Santa. That, my friend, is why I'm here. Now, I understand from Al that your present sleigh has seen better days, is that right?

SANTA   Well, actually I think it's holding up rather well.

**LOU**       Uh-huh. Uh-huh. And is that good enough for you, Santa? Is a sleigh that's merely "holding up rather well" good enough for Father Christmas? I don't think so. No, I think you deserve better than that. I mean, my grandmother is holding up rather well but I'm not about to load her up with toys and drive her around the world. Do you understand what I'm saying, Santa? We cannot have Kris Kringle riding around in a jalopy. I mean, what is this, Chitty Chitty Bang Bang? Come on. How's that gonna look? People hear something rattling overhead, they look up, they see your rusted-out old sleigh bumping along, backfiring, paint chipping off. I tell you, that's not my Santa Claus. No sir. *(He takes out a brochure.)* My Santa Claus rides in a shiny, brand-new, fully loaded Rocket Sleigh.

**SANTA**     Rocket Sleigh?

**LOU**       It's the top of the line, Santa. It's the Cadillac of sleighs. And you deserve nothing but the best. You see what it's got here? Look. It's got disc brakes, power steering, a sound system like you wouldn't believe, air conditioning—all right, you won't need that. We'll take that out—it's got a wide base so you won't tip over when you land on those slanted roofs. And it's got a keyless entry system.

**SANTA**     Keyless entry system?

**LOU**       That's right.

**SANTA**     But it doesn't have any doors.

**LOU**       Exactly.

**SANTA**     Well, it looks very nice, but…

**LOU**       And you know what, Santa? I haven't even mentioned the most impressive feature of this sleigh.

**SANTA**     What's that?

**LOU**       You don't need the reindeer.

**SANTA**     What?

**LOU**       Not so much as an antler! This baby is self-powered. It'll go from zero to Mach three in twenty seconds. I mean, you hitch the reindeer to the front of this machine, they'll be getting a sleigh wedgie!

**SANTA**     Well, Mr. Flapdoodle…

**LOU**       Lou. Call me Lou.

**SANTA**     Well, Lou, I can't have a sleigh with no reindeer. My reindeer wait all year for this trip. The boys and girls love the reindeer. Why, they leave carrots for them every Christmas Eve.

**LOU**       So now they can leave a can of transmission fluid. What's the difference?

**SANTA**     No, I'm sorry, but if the reindeer can't be involved, then I'm afraid I have no use for it.

LOU Well now hold on a second. Hold on. Let's not do something we're both going to regret here, Santa. I mean, if that's going to be a deal breaker then we can work around it. I mean, who says you have to engage the engine? You don't want to use it, don't use it. Let the reindeer pull the sleigh if that's what you want. You're still going to get a smoother ride, softer landings, and a roomy interior. And hey, unless I miss my guess, a gentleman of your exaggerated dimensions is going to need plenty of room. You know what I'm sayin'?

SANTA Well, thanks for pointing that out, Lou, but I think I'll just stick with my old sleigh.

LOU All right, Santa, listen. Do me a favour. Do me a favour. At least take a test drive. Will you do that for me?

SANTA No, I'm afraid I don't have time.

LOU It's parked right outside. The engine's running. Do you hear it?

SANTA No, I don't.

LOU Of course you don't! That's how quiet it is!

SANTA Well, I'm sorry but I have to drop in on choir practice right now.

LOU No problem. I can wait. I'll be right here when you get back.

SANTA Well, I don't know how long I'll be gone.

LOU That's all right. I've got no place to be.

SANTA Well, the choir practice could take a while.

LOU Take all the time you need. I'll just read a periodical. *(He picks up a magazine and sits.)*

SANTA Lou, can't you tell that I'm trying to get rid of you?

LOU I sure can. I hear that every day.

SANTA And yet you insist on staying.

LOU Unbelievable, isn't it?

SANTA All right, I'll tell you what. Why don't you come with me to hear the choir?

LOU Choir, huh? They gonna be singing?

SANTA Well, they're a choir.

LOU Okay, tell me this. If I come with, will you take a test drive afterwards?

SANTA If I have time we'll talk about it.

LOU Talk about it, or do it? I mean, we could talk about it all day long, but you're not going to experience the beauty of this machine until you sit your size forty-eight stocky in the driver's seat.

| | |
|---|---|
| SANTA | Fine, I'll take a test drive after we hear the choir. |
| LOU | All right. What are we waiting for? |
| SANTA | Good. In fact, I'd like to get an outsider's opinion of the choir. |
| LOU | Well, I'm your man then. |
| SANTA | Do you sing? |
| LOU | Do I sing? Does Peter Pan scuba dive? |
| SANTA | No. |
| LOU | Exactly! |

*SANTA and LOU exit. Lights down.*

## ACT ONE Scene Six

*Time: A few minutes later.*

*Place: The workshop.*

*As the lights come up we see the ELVES working at their stations. AL, KIT, and BOZIDAR enter from outside carrying supplies of milk, vinegar, and baking soda. They carry the supplies in and then exit to BOZIDAR's room. SANTA and LOU enter.*

| | |
|---|---|
| SANTA | Very good work, my elves. Very nice indeed. |
| ELVES | Thank you, Santa. |
| SANTA | Everyone, I'd like you to meet another visitor this morning. This is Mr. Flapdoodle. |
| ELVES | Hello, Mr. Flapdoodle. |
| LOU | Hi. How are you? |

*He moves about the room handing out business cards.*

Good to see you. If you're ever in the market for a sleigh, give me a call. *(to the smallest ELF)* And don't worry. We can fix you up with a booster seat.

*The small ELF starts to go after LOU but two other ELVES hold him/her back. AL enters, followed by KIT and BOZIDAR. They don't see SANTA.*

| | |
|---|---|
| AL | Okay, one more trip oughta do it. Then we'll have everything we need. |
| SANTA | Al? |
| AL | Not now, Santa. I'm very busy. |

*AL exits. KIT and BOZIDAR stop. AL enters again.*

Santa! What are you doing here?

**SANTA**    I'm here to listen to the choir. What are you doing?

**AL**    Me? Well, I was just... uh... helping Bozidar with something.

**SANTA**    With what?

**AL**    Well, he's... uh... he's stocking up on eggnog. You see, he doesn't want to run out over the holidays.

**SANTA**    Is that right, Bozidar?

**BOZIDAR**    I am clueless.

**AL**    Bozidar, help me get some chairs for everyone.

*AL and BOZIDAR exit to get chairs.*

**SANTA**    *(to KIT)* Oh, Kit, I'd like you to meet someone. This is Lou Flapdoodle. He's a sleigh salesman from Detroit.

**LOU**    Nice to meet you.

**KIT**    Flapdoodle?

**LOU**    That's right.

**KIT**    Why am I not surprised?

*AL and BOZIDAR enter carrying a few chairs.*

**AL**    Here we go everyone. Everybody have a seat now. There we go.

*People begin to sit. The CHOIR enters.*

Oh, look, it's the choir. Well, it's about time. Come on in, choir! Come right in. Let's go. Move it, move it. March. March! Hiyup!

*AL marches in place and does a rhythmic chant that boot camp soldiers often march to.*

Choir's gonna do its thing! Santa wants to hear it sing! Sound off! *(He stops marching in place.)* Come on. There we go. That's it. Thank you. All right, Santa, they're all yours.

**SANTA**    Thank you. We're here this morning to see how the choir is progressing. Now as most of you know, the choir performs every year at the Christmas Eve wrap party. It is the highlight of our Christmas season here at the North Pole and we all look forward to it very much. And this morning we're lucky enough to have two visitors with us who can also lend an ear. Kit Bishop and Lou Flapdoodle.

**LOU**    *(standing)* National Sleigh Company. If it runs on snow, we make it go. If it runs on gas, then you can ki—

SANTA  All right, thank you, Lou. Choir, I'll turn the floor over to you now. Let's hear how it's coming along.

*SANTA sits. The CHOIR begins to sing "O Come All Ye Faithful." It is not good.*

CHOIR  O come all ye faithful, joyful and triumphant,

O come ye, O come ye to Bethlehem.

Come...

*SANTA holds up his hand for the choir to stop. There is silence.*

SANTA  Well, thank you very much ladies and gentlemen. Thank you. I'm sure I speak for everyone here when I say I don't think we've ever heard anything quite like it. You may return to the rehearsal hall now and continue with your practice. And you might want to think about working right through lunch. Thank you. I look forward to seeing you again on Christmas Eve.

*The CHOIR exits. SANTA turns to the others.*

Well, any comments?

LOU  Well, I'm tone deaf but it sounded good to me.

SANTA  Any skilled comments?

AL  Well, it sounded a tad rough, Santa.

KIT  A tad rough? I've heard nicer sounds out of a whoopee cushion.

SANTA  Uh-huh. Well, I'm afraid I have to agree with Kit. I am going to have to find someone to take over as choirmaster, and the sooner the better. Kit. You're it.

KIT  What?

SANTA  Well you're a music lover, aren't you? You're a singer. You would certainly know more about it than any of us. So you're the new choirmaster. You can take over immediately.

KIT  Oh, now wait a minute. I don't even work here.

SANTA  Yes you do. You're the choirmaster.

KIT  But I didn't agree to it.

SANTA  Didn't agree to it? Phooey!

PHOOEY  Yes, Santa?

SANTA  No, Phooey. Not you. I'm sorry, Kit. I don't ask people to agree to the jobs I assign. If I ran the North Pole that way, we'd still be waiting for our first hula hoop to roll off the assembly line. No, I prefer to take the bull by the horns and make those decisions on my own. Now you get over to the rehearsal hall and whip that choir into shape.

KIT   But, what if I'm not good enough?

SANTA  Not good enough? Fiddlesticks!

FIDDLE-
STICKS  Yes, Santa?

SANTA  No, I didn't mean you, Fiddlesticks. I was… never mind. *(to KIT)* Now what do you mean, "not good enough"?

KIT   Well what if I can't pull it off? What if I fail?

SANTA  Well you won't know unless you try, now will you?

KIT   Well what kind of encouragement is that? You're supposed to tell me that I am good enough.

SANTA  No, you're supposed to show me that you're good enough.

KIT   There you go again. This is not helping.

SANTA  Kit, just go and give it a try. If you succeed, wonderful. If you fail, well, the wrap party is ruined and we all have a horrible Christmas Eve. *(beat)* I'm kidding. Go. You'll be fine. Lou, you come with me. Let's see what this sleigh of yours can do.

LOU   You bet, Santa.

SANTA  Everyone else, back to work. We've only got two days left until Christmas Eve!

    *SANTA and LOU exit to the outside.*

AL    *(to KIT as he pulls out a piece of paper)* Okay listen, you're sure this glue formula will work, huh?

KIT   Yeah, yeah. Just do exactly what I wrote down.

AL    Okay Bozidar, let's get the rest of the ingredients and get to work. Oh, and we have to get some eggnog too.

BOZIDAR Eggnog? Why?

AL    Because I told Santa we were getting eggnog. Do you think I'm going to lie to the big wheel?

BOZIDAR The what?

AL    The big wheel. The big cheese. Santa Claus.

BOZIDAR Santa Claus is big wheel?

AL    He's the biggest wheel. Now, go.

    *BOZIDAR exits to the outside.*

ELVES  Goodbye, Mr. Kidneystone.

AL    Hey, I've got all of your names and I know where you live!

> *AL exits to the outside. The ELVES laugh hysterically. OCTAVIA enters from the elves' quarters.*

**OCTAVIA**  All right. What did I tell you elves about using the laundry hamper for a basketball hoop? And what happens? I go in there and I find dirty clothes all over the place again. Now this has got to stop. Do you hear me?

**ELVES**  Yes, Octavia.

**OCTAVIA**  All right, now off you go and pick them up.

> *The ELVES exit to their quarters. OCTAVIA turns to KIT.*

Do you believe those little rascals? They're always up to some sort of mischief.

**KIT**  I take it you don't like the elves.

**OCTAVIA**  What?

**KIT**  Well, the way you yell at them. Scolding them like that. My mother does that to me too and it makes me wonder if she even likes me sometimes.

**OCTAVIA**  No, I love the elves.

**KIT**  You do?

**OCTAVIA**  Of course I do. That's why I scold them. You have to teach them some manners. You have to teach them what's right and wrong. And you do that because you care and you want them to be the best people they can be. If I didn't love them, it wouldn't matter to me what they did.

**KIT**  Oh.

**OCTAVIA**  Yes, don't you worry. I'm sure your mother feels lucky to have a daughter like you. And your brother's lucky too. I never had a sister, but I always wanted one. I was kind of lonely growing up.

**KIT**  How did you know I had a brother?

**OCTAVIA**  I read his letter.

**KIT**  You what?

**OCTAVIA**  Well... uh... I was dusting Santa's desk and the letter was there and I had to pick it up and move it and as I did I accidentally read some of it.

**KIT**  Oh.

**OCTAVIA**  Your brother sounds very sweet. Not many children are unselfish enough at Christmastime to ask for some Christmas spirit for their sister.

**KIT**  What?

**OCTAVIA**  In the letter. That's what your brother asked for. He.... Oh no. You didn't know. Oh me and my big mouth. When will I learn? Listen, don't tell Santa Claus, all right? Because he doesn't like people snooping. Especially around Christmastime.

**KIT**      Snooping? I thought you said you were dusting.

**OCTAVIA**  Snooping. Dusting. Same thing. Just promise me you won't tell Santa Claus.

**KIT**      *(She holds out her pinky finger.)* Don't worry. I won't tell.

**OCTAVIA**  *(She wraps her pinky finger around KIT's.)* Oh thank you. Thank you. Well, I'd better get back to work.

**KIT**      Uh... Octavia?

**OCTAVIA**  Yes?

**KIT**      Could you tell me where Santa keeps his sleigh?

**OCTAVIA**  His sleigh? Oh, I don't think I could, no. You see, Santa Claus is very protective about his sleigh.

**KIT**      Oh I know he is. In fact, he's so used to being protective, that he forgot to tell me where it is when he asked me to polish it.

**OCTAVIA**  Polish it?

**KIT**      Yes, he asked me to polish the sleigh for Christmas Eve. I guess that's going to be my job while I'm here.

**OCTAVIA**  Oh, I see. Yes, Santa likes everyone to contribute. Even visitors, I guess.

**KIT**      Yeah. Well, he was pretty insistent about me doing this job, and it's hard to say no to Santa Claus.

**OCTAVIA**  Oh I know that. Well, the sleigh is in barn number twelve. Out that door and to your left.

**KIT**      Are the reindeer in there too? Because Santa wanted me to groom them.

**OCTAVIA**  Yes, they're in there too.

**KIT**      Okay. Thanks.

**OCTAVIA**  You're welcome.

> *KIT exits outside.*

Well, isn't that nice. I guess she's getting into the spirit of the season after all.

> *OCTAVIA exits to her quarters. Off, we hear the ELVES giggle. The ELVES enter and move downstage.*

**ELVES**    I don't think so.

> *One of the ELVES throws some pixie dust at the radio. An up-tempo song of the day comes on and the ELVES begin to bop and groove. The ELVES exit dancing. Lights down.*

> *End Act One.*

## ACT TWO Scene One

*Time: A half an hour later.*

*Place: The workshop.*

*Lights up. The ELVES are working and humming a Christmas song. SANTA enters the workshop. He is looking very dishevelled and his hair has been blown back. He is shaky on his feet. LOU enters.*

**LOU**     I'm sorry, Santa. I thought you were used to going fast. I'll have to make a note to get a windshield installed. Here, maybe you'd better sit down.

*LOU helps SANTA to a seat.*

**SANTA**     Do you honestly expect me to drive that contraption? At that speed?

**LOU**     No, Santa, like I said, you don't have to use the engine. You can hitch the reindeer to it and fly at a leisurely Mach one.

**SANTA**     No, I'm afraid that sleigh is just too dangerous.

**LOU**     Too dangerous? It's got seat belts. And it's got air bags too. Oh, and get this. When the air bags open up, they play "White Christmas." Yeah. It's like, boom!

*He begins to sing, SANTA cuts him off.*

**SANTA**     Lou? I'm sorry. I'm afraid you've made the trip up here for nothing.

**LOU**     Now, hang on now, Santa, I'll tell you what. I'll throw in an ice scraper at no charge.

**SANTA**     Now why would I need an ice scraper with no windshield?

**LOU**     For your beard.

**SANTA**     Lou, I think you're just going to have to take no for an answer this time.

**LOU**     Aw, Santa, please? You won't reconsider?

**SANTA**     I'm afraid not.

**LOU**     Oh.

**SANTA**     I think I'll just go with my old sleigh.

**LOU**     Boy, this comes as quite a shock. I'm not used to this. I don't know what I'm going to tell my wife and kids. I mean, those kids are pretty proud of their old man. And now I've gotta go and tell them that I got turned down. By Santa Claus no less. Mr. Soft Touch.

**SANTA**     Lou, I'm sorry.

**LOU**     No, it's not your fault. I just didn't have my good stuff today. Hey, I guess even Lucky Lou Flapdoodle's gotta lose one once in a while. I just hope little Mary and Lou Junior understand that.

**SANTA**     I'm sure they will.

**LOU**     Right. Right. Well, I suppose I'll be heading back then.

**SANTA**     You can still stay for the wrap party if you like. You're more than welcome.

**LOU**     No, I'm afraid I wouldn't be in a partying mood, Santa. No, I'll just shove off. Head home. To the family. I've got a snapshot here if you'd like to see them. *(He takes out his wallet.)* Huh? Here we go. Look at those little faces. Doesn't that break your heart? It's like they're saying, "Santa, buy a sleigh from Daddy."

**SANTA**     Lou?

**LOU**     Well, it was worth a try. *(He puts the picture away.)* Listen, is there a place where I can grab a cup of hot chocolate before I go? Maybe a latte to warm myself up for the trip?

**SANTA**     Oh, certainly. Right across the way here at the cafeteria.

**LOU**     Good. Thanks. Well, it was nice meeting you, Santa. I'm sorry we couldn't do business.

**SANTA**     It was nice seeing you too, Lou. And have a merry Christmas.

**LOU**     Yeah, you too.

     *LOU exits to the outside. OCTAVIA enters. She is sweeping and singing a Christmas song. She looks at SANTA's hair for a beat.*

**OCTAVIA**     I think you're over-moussed.

**SANTA**     What? Oh, it was that ride in that rocket sleigh. *(He begins to fix his hair.)* I knew I should have said no.

**OCTAVIA**     Here, let me help.

**SANTA**     Thank you, Octavia.

**OCTAVIA**     *(straightening SANTA's hair)* Did you ever think of getting a trim?

**SANTA**     Never mind. My hair is fine.

**OCTAVIA**     Sure it is, Santa. That's why we love you. You don't care about fashion trends.

     *Off, we hear the ELVES giggle. The ELVES enter.*

**SANTA**     All right, you little scamps. Back to work. Well, I suppose I should get over to the rehearsal hall and see how Kit is doing.

**OCTAVIA**     Rehearsal hall?

SANTA     Yes. I've put Kit in charge of the choir. I'm hoping she can pass along some of those vocal skills of hers.

OCTAVIA   I thought you put her in charge of the sleigh.

SANTA     The sleigh? No. Whatever gave you that idea?

OCTAVIA   She did.

SANTA     What?

OCTAVIA   She told me you wanted her to polish the sleigh for Christmas Eve. She's out in barn number twelve right now.

SANTA     She's what? She's polishing my sleigh? But that's Bozidar's job. Polishing the sleigh is very delicate work. You have to use just the right amount of polish and just the right counter-clockwise motion. It's a very precise job. And how did she know the sleigh was in barn number twelve?

OCTAVIA   Uh... boy, that's a good question.

SKIFFLE   Octavia told her.

SANTA     What?

OCTAVIA   (to SKIFFLE) Thanks for your help.

SANTA     Why would you tell her that, Octavia?

OCTAVIA   Well, it's a long story. You see...

          *Off, we hear a loud crash.*

SANTA     What on earth was that?

OCTAVIA   It sounded like it came from barn number... from out there somewhere.

SANTA     It sounded to me like it came from barn number twelve.

OCTAVIA   Well Santa, how can you be sure about what you're hearing? I mean, with all that hair over your ears.

          *SANTA goes to the door and looks out.*

          *(to herself)* Oh boy, I'm in trouble.

SANTA     Oh sweet merciful jingle bells. Octavia, have you seen Algernon?

OCTAVIA   I sure have. Three times.

SANTA     Well, if you see him again, tell him there may be a change in this afternoon's schedule.

OCTAVIA   Why's that?

SANTA     Well, from here it looks like my sleigh has just come through the barn wall! But, then again, maybe all that hair is covering my eyes too!!

          *SANTA exits.*

**OCTAVIA**  Oh, I am so in trouble.

*AL enters from BOZIDAR's quarters. He is wearing an industrial-type apron.*

**AL**  Octavia, did I just hear a crash?

**OCTAVIA**  Oh dear, yes. It came from barn number twelve.

**AL**  What happened?

*AL goes to the exit.*

**OCTAVIA**  Well, Santa says it looks like his sleigh went through the barn wall.

**AL**  It what? *(He looks out.)* Holy guacamole!

**OCTAVIA**  I'm afraid to look. Does it look bad?

**AL**  Oh, it looks bad all right. Oh my. *(thinking to himself)* I'd better finish up my work and get out there!

*He starts for BOZIDAR's room.*

**OCTAVIA**  What are you working on?

**AL**  Uh, Bozidar and I are in the middle of something, that's all.

**OCTAVIA**  In the middle of what?

**AL**  Well, I'm afraid I can't tell you, Octavia. It's a secret, and I think the fewer people who know about it, the better off we all are.

**SKIFFLE**  They're making wood glue.

**OCTAVIA**  What? Is that true?

**AL**  Well, yes it is, yes.

**OCTAVIA**  Why would you be making wood glue?

**AL**  No reason. We just thought we'd try our hand at it.

**SKIFFLE**  The supply train didn't bring any.

**OCTAVIA**  What?!

**AL**  *(looks at SKIFFLE)* I should have known with ears like that. Isn't it time for your break? Huh? *(to all the ELVES)* Go on. Take a break.

**ELVES**  Yes, Mr. Headstone.

*The ELVES giggle and exit.*

**AL**  Yeah, enjoy your Mini-Wheats.

**OCTAVIA**  Algernon, how are the elves going to make the toys without wood glue?

AL        Don't worry. We'll have plenty of glue. Bozidar and I are just finishing up the first batch. Now, I have to get back in there, and please Octavia, not a word about this to Santa Claus, all right?

OCTAVIA    Oh, Algernon, don't ask me to lie to Santa. I'm already on thin ice with him.

AL        No, I'm not asking you to lie. I wouldn't do that. I'm just asking you to avoid the truth, that's all. I gotta get back.

*He moves towards BOZIDAR's room.*

OCTAVIA    Oh, Algernon?

AL        *(stopping)* Yes?

OCTAVIA    This is four times now.

AL        Four times? Four times what?

OCTAVIA    Four times we've seen each other today.

AL        Oh, is it? I didn't know. Well, back to work.

*AL exits to BOZIDAR's quarters.*

OCTAVIA    *(to herself)* Didn't know? How could he not know? Am I invisible?

*SANTA enters with KIT.*

Oh Santa Claus. Is everything all right?

SANTA     Well, if you call a hole in the barn, a ruined sleigh, and nine traumatized reindeer all right, then yes, everything is perfect. Kit, you'd better sit down.

*KIT sits.*

OCTAVIA    Is she hurt?

SANTA     No, she's just a little shaken up, that's all.

OCTAVIA    Well, what happened?

SANTA     Well, that's what we're about to find out. Kit, would you mind telling me what you were trying to do out there?

KIT       I was trying to get home.

SANTA     You were trying to get home? With my reindeer and sleigh?

KIT       Well, I didn't have any choice. The train's not going back. I was stuck.

SANTA     But you don't have any experience handling a sleigh. You could have been injured out there. The reindeer could have been hurt.

KIT       You know this isn't all my fault. I mean, the problem is those reindeer don't know how to go in reverse.

SANTA    I know they don't. That's why we have doors at both ends of the barn.

KIT    Oh.

SANTA    And why are you in such a rush to get home? I told you I'd get you home in time for Christmas.

KIT    I need to see my brother.

SANTA    Michael? Why?

KIT    I want to tell him that I'm fine. That he doesn't have to worry about me not having any Christmas spirit.

SANTA    What?

KIT    In his letter. He asked you to give me some Christmas spirit.

        *OCTAVIA begins to back away.*

SANTA    How do you know what was in his letter? Octavia? Where are you going?

OCTAVIA    Nowhere. I was just seeing if I could go in reverse. *(She backs up and moves forward a couple of times.)* Oh, yep. I guess I can. Everything's fine.

SANTA    Do you know anything about these goings on?

OCTAVIA    Me? How would I know what goes on around here? I mean it's not like I live here.

SANTA    You do live here.

OCTAVIA    Darn!

KIT    It's not her fault. I tricked her into telling me where you keep your sleigh.

SANTA    Is that right? And I suppose you tricked her into telling you what was in Michael's letter too.

OCTAVIA    No, Santa, she didn't trick me. I just blurted that out. My big mouth opened up and out it came like somebody opened a sluice gate. It just poured right out of me. It was like yakada-yakada-yakada. I guess I just don't know when to be quiet.

SANTA    …Now would be a good time.

KIT    Don't blame her. It wasn't her fault. She didn't know that I hadn't read the letter.

SANTA    Oh I'm not blaming anybody.

OCTAVIA    That's right. Santa Claus doesn't cast blame. Casting blame solves nothing, right Santa? Blame is like a movie. It should never be miscast.

SANTA    Blame is like a movie?

**OCTAVIA**   I just made it up.

**SANTA**   No kidding. *(to KIT)* Octavia is right about one thing though, Kit. Casting blame does not solve anything. I must say I'm a little disappointed though. I mean, I put you in charge of the choir. That's a very important job.

**KIT**   Oh come on. You didn't care about what kind of a job I did with the choir. You just wanted me to work with them because you thought it might give me some Christmas spirit and then you'd have the answer to my brother's Christmas wish.

**SANTA**   Gee, that's a good idea. I wish I'd thought of it. But the fact is I put you in charge of the choir because you're the most qualified person here.

**KIT**   Really?

**SANTA**   Yes. You're a talented young lady, and I thought some of that talent might rub off on the choir.

**KIT**   You think I'm talented?

**SANTA**   Well, you sure bowled 'em over at your school's talent show last year.

**KIT**   You know about that?

**SANTA**   Kit, eventually, I find out about everything. Isn't that right, Octavia?

**OCTAVIA**   That's right. *(to KIT)* He's like a nosey neighbour. *(to SANTA)* Only not really nosey. *(to KIT)* Or neighbourly.

**SANTA**   Perhaps another reason you're anxious to leave here is that you don't think you can handle the job of choirmaster. Is that a possibility?

**KIT**   I don't know. Maybe.

**SANTA**   I thought so. Well, fine then. Don't worry about it. I'll find someone else. I didn't mean to put you on the spot like that. I'm sorry. Octavia?

**OCTAVIA**   Yo.

**SANTA**   You're the new choirmaster.

**OCTAVIA**   What?!

**SANTA**   And I think you should get started right away.

**OCTAVIA**   Me?

**SANTA**   Yes, you.

**OCTAVIA**   But Santa, I'm your... what do I do here again?

**SANTA**   Housekeeper.

**OCTAVIA**   Right! What do I know from choirs?

**SANTA**    Octavia, I have total and complete confidence in you. I'm sure you'll make a fine choirmaster.

**KIT**    All right. I'll do it.

**OCTAVIA**    Attagirl!

**SANTA**    Are you sure?

**KIT**    Yes. But I'm not making any promises. I mean, I might make them worse than they are. All right, that's not possible. But they might not be any better.

**SANTA**    All I ask is that you try. That's all that we can ask of anybody. Now, you can get started as soon as your head clears.

> *AL enters, followed by BOZIDAR. They have pieces of paper and assorted objects stuck to their clothing.*

**AL**    Oh, Santa, you're here. We were just heading outside to help. Is everything okay?

> *SANTA says nothing. He is looking at the objects stuck to their clothes.*

What is it, Santa? What's wrong?

**SANTA**    Well, you appear to have something stuck to you.

**AL**    Hmm? *(pulling a piece of paper off of his clothing)* Oh! How'd that get there?

> *He tries to get rid of the paper, but it keeps sticking. He finally holds it out to BOZIDAR but their hands get stuck together. They try to free themselves but wind up standing there holding hands, trying to act nonchalant.*

There we go. So. How's it going?

**SANTA**    Al, I'm afraid we have to cancel those appearances I was supposed to make this afternoon.

**AL**    Oh no.

**SANTA**    Yes, my sleigh is in need of some major repairs I'm afraid, and there's no way they can be done by this afternoon.

**AL**    All right then. I'll clear your schedule for you.

> *AL and BOZIDAR turn to leave.*

**SANTA**    Thank you. Bozidar?

> *BOZIDAR stops and turns back to SANTA. AL gets halted in the process.*

**BOZIDAR**    Yes, Santa.

**SANTA**     How long would it take to repair two broken runners, a cracked chassis, and a broken tie rod?

**BOZIDAR**   Oh, Santa Claus, it would take a month of ice cream sundaes to do all that. We have to send out for parts, we have to get them here, and then the labour? To get fixed in time for Christmas, you are dreaming the impossible dream.

**SANTA**     So what are you saying, Bozidar? Are you saying I won't have my sleigh for Christmas Eve?

**BOZIDAR**   You ain't just whistling Dixie Cups.

**OCTAVIA**   Oh my stars. Santa Claus, the boys and girls are expecting you. What are you going to do?

*LOU enters carrying a cup of hot chocolate.*

**LOU**     So, Santa, am I mistaken or is that what used to be a sleigh sticking out of the side of your barn?

**SANTA**     No, Lou, you're not mistaken.

**LOU**     I thought so. Well, gotta fly. *(He turns to leave.)*

**SANTA**     Lou?

**LOU**     *(stopping)* Yes, Santa?

**SANTA**     I was wondering if I could use your sleigh on Christmas Eve.

**LOU**     Use? You mean as in borrow? You don't want to buy it?

**SANTA**     Well, I would only be using it the one time.

**LOU**     Yeah, but that one time, Santa, you're putting on a lot of miles. I mean, flying around the world like that, that's going to depreciate the value. And all those stops and starts? Landing, taking off. Landing, taking off. Landing, taking off. Landing, taking off. Landing—

**SANTA**     Fine. Fine. I get your point.

**LOU**     Well, that's a lot of wear and tear, Santa. All that weight coming down on the runners like that.

**SANTA**     Yes, I know the toys weigh a lot.

**LOU**     Right, and then there's the toys.

**SANTA**     Fine. I don't want to be the cause of any business loss for you, so perhaps we can work out a leasing agreement.

**LOU**     Santa, I know we can. *(giving a card to OCTAVIA)* Hi there. The name's Lucky Lou Flapdoodle.

**SANTA**     Now, I've got some appointments I'd like to keep this afternoon. Lou, maybe you can act as my chauffeur for the day. Would you do that?

**LOU**     Santa, I'd be thrilled to help you out.

SANTA    All right, everybody, that's it then. Kit, are you feeling better?

KIT    I'm great. I'm ready to go.

SANTA    All right then, you'd better get over to the rehearsal hall. Everybody else, back to work. We've still got that Christmas Eve deadline to meet.

> *KIT, LOU, and OCTAVIA exit. ALGERNON and BOZIDAR are trying to pull their hands apart.*

Oh, Al?

> *AL and BOZIDAR stop.*

AL    Yes, Santa?

SANTA    How's the wood glue coming?

AL    …Well, it's sticky, that's for sure.

SANTA    Good. Carry on then.

> *SANTA exits.*

AL    *(to BOZIDAR)* How did he know?

> *AL and BOZIDAR both shrug and then exit holding hands. Lights down.*

## ACT TWO Scene Two

> *Time: Christmas Eve.*
>
> *Place: The workshop.*
>
> *As the lights come up, the ELVES are busy wrapping presents. OCTAVIA enters.*

OCTAVIA    *(looking at the presents)* Oh, that's very nice. Very nice indeed. Good work. *(to another ELF)* Now, I think that one needs a bow. Maybe a nice pink one. *(to all of the ELVES)* Oh, this is my favourite night of the year. Christmas Eve. All the toys are made. The presents are being wrapped.

> *The ELVES gather round OCTAVIA, expecting a nice Christmas moment.*

Meanwhile, all of the children are in their homes, tucked in their beds with visions of sugar plums dancing through their heads. If only every night could be Christmas Eve. Wouldn't that be wonderful? Of course, if every night was Christmas Eve it wouldn't be so special, would it? And you wouldn't have time to make the toys. You'd be spending all your time wrapping. And if you couldn't make the toys, you'd have nothing to wrap. And if you had nothing to wrap, the children wouldn't get any Christmas presents. They'd have visions of nothing dancing through their heads. Boy, that was a really dumb idea, wasn't it?

> *The ELVES move away, slightly disappointed. SANTA Claus enters carrying a wrapped parcel.*

SANTA      Merry Christmas Eve!

ELVES      Merry Christmas Eve, Santa.

OCTAVIA   Oh, hello Santa.

SANTA      Hello Octavia. The wrap party is underway I see.

OCTAVIA   It sure is. Don't the presents look nice?

SANTA      Oh, they certainly do. Absolutely beautiful. You know, I wish every night could be Christmas Eve.

OCTAVIA   Naw, that's a dumb idea. *(pointing to the present SANTA is carrying)* I see you've been doing some wrapping yourself, Santa.

SANTA      Well as a matter of fact I have, Octavia. Here, this is for you.

OCTAVIA   For me?

SANTA      That's right.

OCTAVIA   Oh, thank you, Santa, but, I told you, you didn't have to get me a gift.

SANTA      Balderdash!

BALDERDASH          Yes, Santa?

SANTA      No, I… never mind. Octavia, you've been a big help this year and I think you deserve a gift.

OCTAVIA   Well, thank you.

SANTA      You're very welcome. Now, open it.

OCTAVIA   What, now?

SANTA      Yes, go on.

OCTAVIA   But Santa Claus, it's not Christmas yet.

SANTA      Well, let's call this an early Christmas present. Now open it.

OCTAVIA   Well, all right. If you say so. *(She opens the gift.)* Oh, this is so exciting.

SANTA      I just hope you like it. I picked it up in Paris the other day.

> *OCTAVIA opens the box and takes out a dress.*

OCTAVIA   Oh my word. Santa Claus, it's beautiful.

SANTA      You think so?

**OCTAVIA**  Oh, it's gorgeous. I've never seen a dress so beautiful.

**SANTA**  So, then you do like it.

**OCTAVIA**  Oh, I love it. Thank you.

**SANTA**  You're very welcome.

**OCTAVIA**  I'm going to wear it on the very next special occasion that comes along.

**SANTA**  Well, what's wrong with right now?

**OCTAVIA**  Now? Tonight?

**SANTA**  Certainly. What could be more special than Christmas Eve at the North Pole?

**OCTAVIA**  Yes. I guess you're right. Okay. I'll go and put it on right now.

**SANTA**  Splendid. Wonderful.

*OCTAVIA exits to her quarters.*

Oh, I love this job.

*LOU enters from outside.*

**LOU**  The sleigh's all ready, Santa. I've given her the once-over twice. All we have to do now is hitch the reindeer to her and she's ready for the open sky.

**SANTA**  Good. But before we do that, Lou, I've got a little errand I'd like you to run for me.

**LOU**  An errand?

**SANTA**  That's right. We'll see if this sleigh of yours is as fast as I think it is.

**LOU**  You just name it, Santa. What do you want?

**SANTA**  Well, let's step outside and I'll explain. Little elves tend to hear too much sometimes.

*SANTA and LOU exit. BOZIDAR enters from his room.*

**BOZIDAR**  All right! I am all ready for wrap party. Let the wrapping begin. And I mean Christmas present wrapping. Not Snoop Doggy bag rapping. You can bet your Latifa on that.

*AL enters. He is carrying a suitcase.*

Al, my little pal. What is with luggage? You are not going away for Christmas again this year, are you? Say it isn't so.

**AL**  Oh, it most certainly is. In a matter of hours I'm gonna be lyin' on a beach soaking up the sun.

**BOZIDAR**  But Al, it is not right that you are spending Christmas alone. You should spend it here with your friends.

**AL**   Friends? I'm the chief of staff, Bozidar. You don't make many friends being the chief of staff. Besides, Christmas isn't for someone like me. It's for the kids. So it's best that I just get out of it's way.

**BOZIDAR** No, that is wrong. Christmas is for everyone. Is for me, is for you, is for Santa Claus. It's not just about presents for little ones. Is not about presents at all. It is feeling. In here. Inside. It make you feel good. Feel happy like child for one month, one week, even one day. And to feel like that for just one day—like child again—is worth waiting for whole year.

**AL**   Yeah, well, I don't think I know how to feel like that, Bozidar. I don't know if I ever did.

**BOZIDAR** Oh, of course you did. You were child once.

**AL**   No, I was forty years old when I was born.

**BOZIDAR** Al, you are as wrong as rain.

**AL**   Bozidar, I'll be fine, all right? Don't worry about it. And listen, thanks for your help with the wood glue. You did a very commendable job there. Why, if it wasn't for you, we might not have made the deadline this year. Your work was exceptional.

**BOZIDAR** You mean that?

**AL**   Of course I mean it. Why would I say it if I didn't mean it?

**BOZIDAR** But you never give compliment. As long as you have been chief of staff, not once have you given me compliment.

**AL**   Well, you haven't deserved one until now.

**BOZIDAR** Oh I know you don't mean that. You are pulling my leg warmers. That is just your way of acting like king of jungle when deep down you are just pussycat in boots.

**AL**   Well, I doubt that.

**BOZIDAR** No, I know. I know. Underneath that flat exterior of yours is a glossy interior latex.

**AL**   Yeah, whatever.

    *SANTA Claus enters.*

Ah! Santa Claus. I've gone over the pre-flight checklist and it looks like we're a go for liftoff.

**SANTA** Wonderful.

**AL**   All we have to do now is finish wrapping, load the toys, and we're out of here.

**SANTA** Oh, now there's no rush, Al. We've still got plenty of time. We've got a party to enjoy. Plus, we haven't heard the choir yet. We can't leave before we hear the choir.

**AL**     Yeah, well, I wouldn't get my hopes up about the choir, Santa.

**SANTA**     Oh? Why's that?

**AL**     Well, I happen to know that your new choirmaster gave the choir the day off yesterday.

**SANTA**     She what?

**AL**     The entire day. She sat in the rehearsal hall yesterday all by herself.

**SANTA**     What was she doing there?

**AL**     Slacking off would be my guess. But I know for a fact there was no rehearsal. And you heard the choir yourself, Santa. You don't think they need rehearsing? That's like saying Bozidar doesn't need a translator.

**BOZIDAR**     I don't need translator. I understand everything you say as clear as bell-bottom pants.

**SANTA**     Well, what about today? Did the choir rehearse today?

**AL**     Well, yeah, but one day isn't going to turn that sow's ear into a silk purse. In fact, don't be surprised if they don't even show up tonight.

**SANTA**     Yeegads!

**AL**     I know how you feel.

**SANTA**     No, I was talking to one of the elves. *(to YEEGADS)* Yeegads, take the rest of the elves and see if you can find Kit and the choir. Hurry!

*The ELVES exit quickly.*

And look everywhere. Leave no stone unturned!

**BOZIDAR**     Santa Claus, this is terrible. Choir singing is Pinocchio of whole wrap party.

**SANTA**     It's the what?

**AL**     The pinnacle.

**SANTA**     Oh. I can't believe this. I thought if I gave Kit that job, she would rise to the challenge.

**AL**     Santa, how many times do I have to tell you? You've got to run these ideas past me first. That's what I'm here for. I mean, sure you're the boss, but sometimes you take on too much. You get stressed out and you make some questionable decisions. Like the time you gave Wayne Gretzky that baseball mitt for Christmas.

**SANTA**     I thought he'd make a good shortstop.

**AL**     That's what I'm saying. You're not perfect. Nobody is.

*OCTAVIA enters wearing her new dress. AL looks at her.*

Well, almost nobody. Wow. I didn't know Octavia had a sister.

SANTA     Al, that is Octavia.

AL     Get out of town.

SANTA     It is.

BOZIDAR     Well you could knock me over with a pheasant.

SANTA     Well Octavia, how do you like it?

OCTAVIA     It's beautiful Santa Claus. It's the nicest dress I've ever had.

AL     Octavia, you look wonderful.

OCTAVIA     Thank you.

AL     You look stunning.

OCTAVIA     Thanks.

SANTA     Bozidar, why don't you and I help with some of the wrapping? All right?

BOZIDAR     Wrapping?

SANTA     Yes.

BOZIDAR     Oh, right! Wrapping. We use this as lame excuse to leave Al and Octavia alone, huh?

SANTA     ...Right.

BOZIDAR     Good plan, Stan.

> SANTA *and* BOZIDAR *move away and begin wrapping presents.*

OCTAVIA     Is that your suitcase?

AL     Hmm? Oh, yes. Yes it is. I'm all packed and ready to go.

OCTAVIA     Down south.

AL     Right. Well, it is the only direction from here after all.

OCTAVIA     I know. You told me that the other day.

AL     I did?

OCTAVIA     Yes.

AL     Oh.

OCTAVIA     You don't remember?

AL     Oh, sure I do. Sure. We were in Santa's office.

OCTAVIA     We were right here.

AL     We were right here, yes. I remember that.

OCTAVIA   And I said it was too bad you weren't going to be coming to the party.

AL   Well, I'm here.

OCTAVIA   Yes, but you're going to be leaving with Santa Claus.

AL   Well, yes, I am.

OCTAVIA   What's the problem, Algernon? Don't you like spending time with the people here?

AL   I beg your pardon?

OCTAVIA   Is that why you go away every Christmas?

AL   What? No.

OCTAVIA   Is that why you'd rather spend Christmas alone?

AL   No, I just...

OCTAVIA   You just what? You know, there are people here who might feel slighted when you go away every year. They might feel that you don't like me. Them. Us.

AL   Well, I certainly don't mean for that to happen.

OCTAVIA   Then why do you do it? Why do you leave us every Christmas?

AL   Well, Christmas is a time of togetherness.

OCTAVIA   Exactly. That's exactly what I'm saying.

AL   Would you let me finish please? It's a time for socializing. Being friendly. And I've never been much of a social person, you know? I don't really know how to act in social situations. I'm a business person. Socializing doesn't come easy for me.

OCTAVIA   Well, it's not that hard really. You just have to relax.

AL   I don't know how to do that either.

OCTAVIA   Well, I could show you how.

AL   You?

OCTAVIA   Yes. I mean, if you were interested.

AL   Well, I don't know.

OCTAVIA   Fine. Never mind then. If you don't want to cultivate your friendships here then there's really no point, is there?

AL   No, it's not that. It's just... boy, you really look terrific, you know that?

OCTAVIA   Thank you. It's just a shame that it took a pretty dress to get you to notice me.

*OCTAVIA moves away from AL.*

**AL** *(to SANTA and BOZIDAR)* Did I do something wrong? What did I do?

*KIT enters with the ELVES.*

**ELVES** Here she is Santa! Here's Kit!

**SANTA** So they found you, did they?

**KIT** Yeah. Sorry I'm late. We were doing some last minute adjustments.

**SANTA** Last minute. Uh-huh. Well, there were some who didn't think you would show up at all.

**KIT** Why wouldn't I show up? I thought this was a big deal for you people.

**SANTA** Oh, it is. It is. And that's why I don't understand why you didn't rehearse yesterday.

**KIT** Oh, well there was a good reason for that.

**SANTA** And what would that reason be?

**AL** Yeah, I'd like to hear that myself.

**KIT** Well, I spent the day writing a Christmas song for the choir to sing. I mean, I know I caused a lot of trouble here, and you've been pretty good about it, so I thought I should find some way to thank you. So I wrote a song for you.

**SANTA** Oh.

**AL** Boy, Santa, I'll bet you feel bad about doubting her now, huh?

**SANTA** As a matter of fact I do. I'm sorry, Kit. I should have trusted you.

**KIT** Ah, don't worry about it. You're not perfect.

**SANTA** Why does everybody keep saying that?

**KIT** So, where do you want us? Is right here okay?

**SANTA** Uh, yes, yes. But I wonder if you could wait for just a minute or two before getting underway.

**KIT** Why?

**SANTA** Well, I'm expecting a couple of guests for your performance. I'm sure they would love to hear what you've done.

*LOU enters from outside.*

**LOU** Santa! Santa!

**SANTA** Ah, Lou! You made it.

**LOU** Hey, would I let Santa Claus down? Not a chance.

**SANTA**     So did you get them?

**LOU**     I sure did. *(calling out the door)* Come on in, folks!

> *MRS. BISHOP and MICHAEL Bishop enter. Their hair is extremely windswept.*

**KIT**     Mom! Michael!

**SANTA**     Lou, what did you do to these poor people?

**LOU**     Sorry, Santa. I had to open her right up.

> *KIT moves to her mother and MICHAEL, and gives them a hug. Then she helps her mother straighten her hair.*

**BOZIDAR**     Look at that. Such a loving family. That is a sight for four eyes.

**SANTA**     All right now, we haven't got much time everybody. Mrs. Bishop? Michael? I'd be honoured if you would sit over here with me.

> *MRS. BISHOP and MICHAEL move and sit near SANTA Claus. ALGERNON moves to OCTAVIA who is sitting. He points to the seat beside her.*

**AL**     Do you mind if I sit here?

**OCTAVIA**     It's a free country. You can sit wherever you like.

**AL**     Well, I think I'd like to sit here.

**OCTAVIA**     Well, then park it.

**AL**     Thanks.

> *He sits. Everyone else watches them. AL looks at them and they all look away.*

Nice weather we're having.

**OCTAVIA**     It's minus fifty.

**AL**     You see? What did I tell you? I don't know what to say in social situations.

**OCTAVIA**     You don't have to say anything. I mean, it's not like you're trying to impress me.

**AL**     Actually, I am trying to impress you.

**SANTA**     All right Kit, if you'll get the choir ready please.

> *KIT brings the CHOIR in and gets them ready.*

Ladies and gentlemen, each year at the wrap party the North Pole Choir favours us with a lovely Christmas song to send my reindeer and I off on our Christmas Eve journey. This year is very special though, because we have a brand new song written for us by Miss Kit Bishop. Oh, what's the song called, Kit?

**KIT**     "This Is My Christmas."

**SANTA**     "This Is My Christmas." All right then, here is Kit Bishop and the North Pole Choir, with "This Is My Christmas."

*Everyone applauds. The CHOIR sings the song.*

**CHOIR**
Snow falling softly on neighbourhood trees
Children excited about Christmas Eve
Grandmother baking her gingerbread cookies
This is my Christmas. (This is Christmas to me.)

The smell of hot chocolate, a warm fire's glow
Two people kissing beneath mistletoe
Wrapping up presents with ribbons and bows
This is my Christmas. (It's the Christmas I know.)

It's hearing my mother say Santa is coming
It's hearing the sound of a wind-up toy drumming
It's seeing the face of my brother, a face filled with glee.
(This is my Christmas. This is my Christmas.)

It's falling asleep with the reindeer near
It's waking to find that Santa has been here
It's the absolute happiest day of the year.

### *CHORUS*

This is my Christmas
This is my Christmas
This is my Christmas
It's the absolute happiest day of the year.

This is my Christmas
(This is my Christmas)
This is my Christmas
(This is my Christmas)
This is my Christmas
(This is my Christmas)
It's the absolute happiest day of the year.

Ooo,ooo,ooo,oooo
Ooo,ooo,ooo,oooo
Ooo,ooo,ooo,oooo
This is my Christmas.

Greeting card pictures of horses and sleighs
Sent from loved ones far away
Drying our mittens and counting the days
This is my Christmas. (This is Christmas to me.)

Hanging up stockings and trimming the tree
Alastair Sim playing Scrooge on TV
Christmas lights dancing on every street
This is my Christmas. (This is Christmas to me.)

It's hearing my mother say Santa is coming
It's hearing the sound of a wind-up toy drumming
It's seeing the face of my brother, a face filled with glee.
(This is my Christmas. This is my Christmas.)

It's falling asleep with the reindeer near
It's waking to find that Santa has been here
It's the absolute happiest day of the year.

### CHORUS

This is my Christmas
This is my Christmas
This is my Christmas
It's the absolute happiest day of the year.

This is my Christmas
(This is my Christmas)
This is my Christmas
(This is my Christmas)
This is my Christmas
(This is my Christmas)

It's the absolute happiest day of the year
It's the absolute happiest day of the year
It's the absolute happiest day
This is my Christmas!

*The song ends. Everyone applauds. SANTA stands.*

**SANTA**     Kit, I don't think I could ask for a better send-off on this night of joy and celebration. Thank you. It sounds to me like you've really found the Christmas spirit.

*KIT and MICHAEL hug.*

Oh, there is one thing though.

| | |
|---|---|
| **KIT** | What's that? |
| **SANTA** | Well, you're not wearing your hat. |
| **KIT** | What hat? |
| **SANTA** | What hat? Oh my. *(to the others)* She doesn't know about the hat, everyone. How could you not know about the hat? |
| **KIT** | Well, nobody told me about it. |
| **SANTA** | Oh well, let me tell you then. When it's Christmastime at the North Pole everybody wears the hat. It's part of the seasonal costume. |

> *SANTA pulls the hat out of his coat.*

Here you go.

| | |
|---|---|
| **KIT** | What's this? |
| **SANTA** | That's the hat. |
| **KIT** | I'm supposed to wear this? |
| **SANTA** | Oh yes. It's tradition. Now, go ahead. Put it on. |
| **KIT** | Really? |
| **SANTA** | Yes. |
| **KIT** | All right. But it's going to look silly. |
| **SANTA** | Oh no it won't. Go ahead. |

> *KIT puts the hat on, it's too big and everyone laughs.*

| | |
|---|---|
| **BOZIDAR** | I love that bit. |
| **KIT** | That's great. So you're making fun of me now. |
| **OCTAVIA** | Oh no, Kit. Not at all. This means you've been accepted. |
| **KIT** | It does? |
| **OCTAVIA** | Oh yes. |
| **AL** | It does? |
| **SANTA** | Of course it does. You didn't know? |
| **AL** | Sure I knew. I knew all along. |
| **SANTA** | All right, Bozidar, are the reindeer hitched up? |
| **BOZIDAR** | The pit crew was standing by, Santa. They should be all set for you. |
| **SANTA** | Good. Well let's get those presents out there with the rest of them, everyone. It's time to go. |

> *The ELVES carry the presents outside. BOZIDAR takes some presents out too.*

That's it. There we go.

LOU     *(looking at the elves)* Look at them. They're so cute. I'd like to take one of them home to meet my kids.

AL     Take two. They're small.

SANTA     Michael, thank you so much for your letter. That was a very special wish you had. Your mother can be very proud of you. And of your sister too. Yes, you and Kit have made this a Christmas that we will always remember up here at the North Pole. And I want you to remember it as well. Forever. I want you to keep it in your heart where it will be safe. And years from now when you have children of your own, and they ask you the meaning of Christmas, you can open up your heart and share it with them. Will you do that for me?

MICHAEL     Yes, Santa.

SANTA     That's a good boy. All right, Mrs. Bishop and Michael can ride in the front seat with me. Kit, Lou, and Al, you'll be riding in the back seat with the toys.

*The ELVES enter again. BOZIDAR enters.*

Are the toys all loaded, Bozidar?

BOZIDAR     You bet your bottom they are.

SANTA     I beg your pardon?

AL     Your bottom dollar.

SANTA     Oh. Right. Okay everybody, off we go.

*MRS. BISHOP and MICHAEL exit.*

LOU     Santa, this is the proudest moment of my life. Just imagine. The Christmas gifts are going to be delivered in a sleigh that I sold.

SANTA     Leased.

LOU     Potato, potahto, Santa. Potato, potahto. *(to the others)* Merry Christmas everyone!!

*LOU exits. Everyone shouts goodbye and merry Christmas.*

SANTA     Kit, are you all set?

KIT     Yep. Goodbye everyone. Thanks Bozidar.

*She hugs BOZIDAR.*

BOZIDAR     Goodbye, Kit. You be good, uh? You mind your P's and Q-tips.

KIT     I will. Have a nice Christmas, Octavia.

OCTAVIA     Good luck, Kit.

*She gives KIT a hug.*

KIT          Sorry I got you in trouble.

OCTAVIA      Oh, don't worry about it.

KIT          Sisters? *(She holds out her pinky finger.)*

OCTAVIA      Sisters. *(She wraps her pinky finger around KIT's.)*

KIT          *(to ALGERNON)* And then there's you.

AL           Hey, you don't have to say goodbye to me yet. I'll see you in the sleigh.

KIT          You think so?

AL           Absolutely.

KIT          Yeah, well, just in case. Thanks.

             *KIT moves to hug AL but he puts his hands up to prevent her.*

AL           Yeah, yeah. That's okay. No problem.

KIT          And... uh... here's your ten dollars back.

             *She hands AL ten dollars. SANTA takes the ten dollars from AL and gives it to BOZIDAR.*

Thanks, everybody. I'm really gonna miss this place. Stupid names and all.

             *KIT kisses AL on the cheek and exits.*

ALL          Goodbye, Kit!

SANTA        Algernon? Are you ready?

AL           Yeah. All set. Let's hit the road.

             *AL picks up his suitcase and moves to the door.*

Well, so long everybody. I'll uh... I'll see you back here in a couple of weeks.

BOZIDAR      Goodbye, Al.

OCTAVIA      Have a nice Christmas, Algernon.

AL           Yeah. You too. Have a good one.

             *AL turns to leave.*

ELVES        Goodbye, Mr. Gladstone!

             *AL stops. He looks back at the ELVES. They smile at him.*

AL           You know, Santa, I'm worried that maybe the sleigh is a little too crowded, you know? Maybe I should stay behind to ensure the comfort of the other passengers.

SANTA        Oh, I'm sure there's plenty of room, Al.

AL           You think so?

SANTA    Oh, yes, it's much larger than the old sleigh. There should be no problem fitting you in.

AL        Oh.

SANTA    That's if you really want to go.

AL        Yeah, well, I'm thinking maybe I don't really want to go after all. Maybe I'll just spend Christmas here.

*AL holds out his hand for OCTAVIA. She takes it.*

With my friends.

SANTA    I think that's a wonderful idea. All right then. I guess this is it. I want you all to know that you have done a superb job again this year. It makes me so proud every time I put a child's gift under a Christmas tree, because I know that each gift is the result of a group effort by some very extraordinary people. You make me look awfully good out there, and for that, I thank you. Goodbye, everyone.

OCTAVIA
& AL      Goodbye, Santa!

BOZIDAR   Goodbye, you big wheel of cheese!

SANTA    *(to AL)* What?

AL        I have no idea.

*SANTA exits.*

ALL       Goodbye, Santa! Goodbye!

SANTA    *(off)* On Rudolph! On Dasher! On Dancer! Ho Ho Ho!! Merry Christmas everyone! Merry Christmas!

*Everyone moves down and looks out as if following SANTA and his sleigh with their eyes. They wave.*

ALL       Merry Christmas!

*Lights down.*

*End.*

# The Christmas Tree

*The Christmas Tree* was first produced at the Lunchbox Theatre in Calgary, Alberta, from November 24 to December 30, 2008, with the following cast and production team:

DANIEL                          Christopher Hunt
SONJA                           Heather Lea MacCallum

Director: Martin Fishman
Set and lighting designer: Sandi Somers
Costume designer: Shauna Breslawski
Stage manager: Rikki Schlosser
Apprentice stage manager: Alec McCauley
Assistant director: Scott Roberts
Intern: Belinda Jackson

# ACT ONE

*Time: Christmas Eve.*

*Place: A Christmas tree lot in the city.*

*The stage is bare except for a Christmas tree and a bench.*

*DANIEL enters stage left. He looks at the Christmas tree.*
*SONJA enters stage right. She looks at the Christmas tree. They*
*circle it once or twice.*

**DANIEL**  Hi.

**SONJA**  Hello.

**DANIEL**  How ya doin'?

**SONJA**  Good.

**DANIEL**  Seems odd, huh?

**SONJA**  What seems odd?

**DANIEL**  That we're both looking this Christmas tree up and down like this.

**SONJA**  Why is that odd?

**DANIEL**  Well, it's the only Christmas tree left. It's not like we have any others to choose from, right?

**SONJA**  Right.

**DANIEL**  I guess that's what happens when you wait until Christmas Eve to get your tree. I mean who waits until Christmas Eve to get a Christmas tree? What's the point even? You put it up, you decorate it. Two days later it comes down. It's kindling. It's mulch. It ridiculous, right?

**SONJA**  I suppose.

**DANIEL**  Absolutely. We should just forget it. Save our money.

**SONJA**  Yeah.

**DANIEL**  Yep, that's what I'm gonna do.

*SONJA moves to pick up the tree.*

What? Wait a minute. Wait.

**SONJA**  What's wrong?

**DANIEL**  What are you doing?

**SONJA**  I'm taking the tree.

**DANIEL**  You're what? You're taking the tree?

**SONJA**  I'm taking the tree.

| | |
|---|---|
| DANIEL | But, I was here first. |
| SONJA | So? |
| DANIEL | Well, I should have first dibs on it, don't you think? |
| SONJA | No, I don't think. |

*SONJA grabs the tree.*

| | |
|---|---|
| DANIEL | Wait a minute. Wait. |
| SONJA | What? |
| DANIEL | Well, let's be fair about this. |
| SONJA | I thought you didn't want it. |
| DANIEL | Did I say that? |
| SONJA | You said we should forget it. Save our money. |
| DANIEL | All right, I said that, but… |
| SONJA | You put it up, two days later it comes down. |
| DANIEL | I said that too. |
| SONJA | It's kindling. It's mulch. |
| DANIEL | Yes, thank you. I know what I said. |
| SONJA | So I assumed that you didn't want it. |
| DANIEL | What? How could you jump to that conclusion? That's a bit of a leap, don't you think? |
| SONJA | No, I don't think. |

*SONJA grabs the tree.*

| | |
|---|---|
| DANIEL | All right, wait. Wait. I'll tell you what. I'll flip you for it. |
| SONJA | What? |
| DANIEL | We'll flip a coin to see who gets the tree. |
| SONJA | So you do want it. |
| DANIEL | Yes, I do. |
| SONJA | So I was right. |
| DANIEL | What? |
| SONJA | When I concluded that you wanted the tree. I was right. |
| DANIEL | Is that important to you? That you were right? |
| SONJA | Yes, it is. |
| DANIEL | You need that, do you? The satisfaction of knowing you were right. |

| | |
|---|---|
| SONJA | Yes, I do. |
| DANIEL | Well, maybe I won't give you that satisfaction. |
| SONJA | Suit yourself. |

*SONJA moves with the tree.*

| | |
|---|---|
| DANIEL | All right, wait. Wait! You were right, okay? You were right. |
| SONJA | Thank you. |
| DANIEL | So can we flip for it now? To see who gets it? |
| SONJA | I've already got it. |
| DANIEL | No, you don't. |
| SONJA | I'm holding it, aren't I? |
| DANIEL | *(puts his hand on the tree)* Well, now I'm holding it too. |
| SONJA | *(puts her other hand on the tree)* Well, I'm holding it more. |
| DANIEL | *(puts his other hand on the tree)* No you're not. |
| SONJA | Let go. |
| DANIEL | You let go. |
| SONJA | I had it first. |
| DANIEL | Well, I saw it first. |
| SONJA | Gimme it. |
| DANIEL | No, you gimme it. |
| SONJA | Let go of my tree, you big ape. |
| DANIEL | Oh, that's nice. Calling a person names on Christmas Eve. That's very jolly of you. |
| SONJA | Just let go of the tree, will you please? |
| DANIEL | All right. Wait. Hold it. Hold it! We're adults for heaven's sake. We're not children; we're not school kids; we're not ragamuffins. Let's discuss this. |
| SONJA | Fine. |
| DANIEL | Fine. Now, let go of the tree and we'll talk. |
| SONJA | You let go first. |
| DANIEL | No, you let go first. |
| SONJA | Why should I let go first? I had it first. Now let go. |
| DANIEL | Nuh-uh. |
| SONJA | Oh fine then. Have it your... |

*She looks past DANIEL, faking seeing something.*

Oh my God, look at that.

DANIEL  Nice try but I'm not looking.

SONJA  Your fly's undone.

DANIEL  It's always undone. I like it that way.

SONJA  All right, how about this? We'll both let go on the count of three.

DANIEL  On the count of three?

SONJA  On the count of three.

DANIEL  All right.

SONJA  So when I say three we'll let go. Okay?

DANIEL  Okay. When you say three.

SONJA  When I say three.

DANIEL  Okay.

SONJA  Okay. Here we go. One.

DANIEL  You're not going to let go, are you?

SONJA  No.

DANIEL  Me neither.

SONJA  Well, we can't stand here like this all night.

DANIEL  No, we can't.

SONJA  I've got things to do.

DANIEL  Oh, and I don't? I've got a lot of things to do.

SONJA  So do I.

DANIEL  It's Christmas Eve.

SONJA  Oh, and I don't know that?

DANIEL  I've got places to be.

SONJA  So do I.

DANIEL  People to spend the yuletide with.

SONJA  And I don't have people? I've got lots of people.

DANIEL  I'm sure you do.

SONJA  Of course I do.

DANIEL  So let's a flip a coin and get it over with.

SONJA  ...Oh all right.

*SONJA lets go of the tree.*

**DANIEL**  Good. Thank you.

*DANIEL lets go of the tree.*

Now isn't this better? We're acting like grown-ups finally. Like mature adults instead of hooligans. Instead of rabble rousers. Instead of street thugs.

**SONJA**  Just flip the coin, would you?

**DANIEL**  I'll flip it when I'm ready to flip it. I've got to get it out first, don't I?

**SONJA**  Well, get it out.

**DANIEL**  I'm getting it out, Bossy Boots. *(He takes a coin out of his pocket.)* There, it's out. Okay? Geez.

**SONJA**  So who's going to call it?

**DANIEL**  I don't care who calls it.

**SONJA**  Fine. I'll call it.

**DANIEL**  Why should you call it?

**SONJA**  Well, somebody's gotta call it.

**DANIEL**  But why you? Why can't I call it?

**SONJA**  You said you didn't care who calls it.

**DANIEL**  I don't care who calls it.

**SONJA**  Fine. Then I'm calling it.

**DANIEL**  Fine.

**SONJA**  Fine.

**DANIEL**  I just don't know why it should be you and not me.

**SONJA**  Because I say so.

**DANIEL**  All right. Well, now I know why. Now I understand. Thank you for clearing that up.

**SONJA**  Are you going to flip it or not?

**DANIEL**  I'm going to flip it right now.

**SONJA**  Thank you.

**DANIEL**  Are you going to call it in the air?

**SONJA**  That's how it's usually done, isn't it?

**DANIEL**  Yes it is.

**SONJA**  Then that's how I'm doing it.

**DANIEL**   I just wanted to be sure that you were clear on the flipping protocol.

**SONJA**   I'm clear.

**DANIEL**   Good. All right. You ready?

**SONJA**   I'm ready.

**DANIEL**   So am I. Here goes.

>   *DANIEL flips the coin.*

**SONJA**   Heads.

>   *DANIEL catches the coin but doesn't look at it.*

**DANIEL**   No, wait a minute. Wait.

**SONJA**   What's wrong?

**DANIEL**   You called heads.

**SONJA**   I know I called heads.

**DANIEL**   Well, statistically, heads comes up more often than tails because there is more weight on the heads side of the coin.

**SONJA**   So?

**DANIEL**   So, it's not fair.

**SONJA**   What if I'd called tails?

**DANIEL**   That would have been fine.

**SONJA**   Well, I called heads. So what is it?

**DANIEL**   Okay look, we shouldn't flip a coin. It's too random.

**SONJA**   What is it? Is it heads or tails?

**DANIEL**   Never mind what it is. I'm putting the coin away. *(He puts the coin in his pocket.)*

**SONJA**   Why?

**DANIEL**   Because this is too important to be decided by something as cavalier and happenstance as a coin flip. I mean, it's the last tree.

**SONJA**   Well, it's the last tree here, but there are other tree lots around. In fact, there's another tree lot about four blocks over. Why don't you go there and get a tree?

**DANIEL**   They're all out of trees.

**SONJA**   I know. I was just there.

**DANIEL**   What? You knew they were out of trees and you were going to send me there anyway?

SONJA     I'm sorry.

DANIEL     I would get into my car and drive there and you knew they had no trees?

SONJA     I'm sorry.

DANIEL     I can't believe that. Such deception, and on Christmas Eve too. Shame on you.

SONJA     All right! I'm sorry!

DANIEL     And there is no need to raise our voices either, young lady.

SONJA     Look, this is the last tree for blocks. Maybe for miles.

DANIEL     It might be the last tree in the entire city. In the entire province.

SONJA     Well, I doubt if it's the last tree in the entire province.

DANIEL     I was just trying to make a point.

SONJA     So what are we gonna do?

DANIEL     I'm open to suggestions.

SONJA     …All right. All right.

DANIEL     Have you got an idea?

SONJA     I've got an idea.

DANIEL     Good. Let's have it.

SONJA     I'm going to tell you why I need this tree so badly.

DANIEL     What's that going to accomplish?

SONJA     Well, when you hear my story you'll see that I need this tree more than you do. You'll have sympathy for me and you'll let me have the tree.

DANIEL     I'll have sympathy for you?

SONJA     Yes.

DANIEL     How do you know I'm a sympathetic person? Maybe I'm not. Maybe I'm callous. In fact, I had a woman tell me that once. That I was callous. Yeah, she had this parrot and it was always yapping, you know? It really got on my nerves. So I was at her place one night and things were going along nicely. It was very romantic, and then this parrot starts up. Yap, yap, yap. Completely spoiled the mood. But then all of a sudden, in mid-sentence, the parrot collapsed and died. It was like, "Polly want a arrggg," and it keeled over. Just like that. So I walked over to the cage and I looked at this dead bird lying there and I said, "Polly want a what? Polly want a what?" She didn't think it was funny. So maybe I won't have sympathy for your tale of woe.

SONJA     Well I'll have to take that chance, won't I?

**DANIEL**    All right. Roll the dice.

**SONJA**    Now, I don't like doing this. I don't like laying my pathetic life story on you, but if that's what it's going to take to get this tree then that's what I'm prepared to do. Embarrassing as it may be.

**DANIEL**    Can I sit?

**SONJA**    What?

**DANIEL**    I like to sit when I'm being told a story. A person can't stand and be told a story. They should be sitting. Storytelling is a sitting thing.

**SONJA**    Fine. Sit. Whatever. Man!

**DANIEL**    You've got an attitude problem, you know that? Very big attitude problem.

**SONJA**    Are you going to sit?

**DANIEL**    I'm just saying. It's a shortcoming. Okay?

    *DANIEL sits.*

**SONJA**    Are you ready now?

**DANIEL**    I'm ready.

**SONJA**    All right, here's the story. I'm a single mother.

**DANIEL**    No surprise there.

**SONJA**    What's that supposed to mean?

**DANIEL**    Well, you're a little on the abrasive side.

**SONJA**    Abrasive?

**DANIEL**    That's the impression I get.

**SONJA**    You don't even know me. We just met.

**DANIEL**    And already I think you're abrasive. That should tell you something. You should probably work on that. Then you might not be alone.

**SONJA**    Can I continue?

**DANIEL**    Just an observation. Please, go on.

**SONJA**    I'm a single mother. I work at two jobs so I can support myself and my offspring. And even with two jobs I still don't make enough in today's economy to be able to give them a decent Christmas. They're getting one present each and their stockings will only be half-filled.

**DANIEL**    So buy smaller stockings.

**SONJA**    What?

**DANIEL**    With smaller stockings they'll look full.

**SONJA**     Can I finish my story please?

**DANIEL**     Just trying to help.

**SONJA**     So I figured the least I could do was to get them a Christmas tree, but until I got paid today, I didn't have enough money even for that. That's why I'm here on Christmas Eve. I've got just enough money in my pocket for this tree. And when I get it home we'll have to lean it in a corner because I can't afford a tree stand, and then we'll decorate it with stringed popcorn and angels that we cut out of construction paper, provided I have enough change left over to buy an inexpensive pair of scissors. And we can't leave milk and cookies for Santa Claus tonight because the cupboard is bare. All we can leave him is a gift certificate from Fat Burger that I found in an old jewellery box that I was getting ready to pawn... so I could buy shoes for the little tots.

**DANIEL**     Wow.

**SONJA**     Yeah, wow.

**DANIEL**     That is pathetic.

**SONJA**     I told you.

**DANIEL**     Hmm. Those boots? Are they Botticelli, or Emma Hope?

**SONJA**     I beg your pardon?

**DANIEL**     Emma Hope. Yeah, Emma Hope's a little rougher around the edges. So what do they go for? Three hundred? Three fifty?

**SONJA**     I forget.

**DANIEL**     You forget? As a woman who worries about how much scissors cost, I think you'd remember what you paid for your boots.

**SONJA**     Are you saying you don't believe my story?

**DANIEL**     No I don't. It's a complete fabrication. It's full of holes. First of all, no mother in the world would refer to her children as offspring. Children, kids, brats, pains in the butt, but not something as sterile as offspring. And then there's the boots, the gorgeous hair, the whole look. You've got money and lots of it. Am I right?

**SONJA**     How do you know so much about women's boots?

**DANIEL**     I dated a woman once who had high-class tastes.

**SONJA**     In everything but men obviously.

**DANIEL**     Obviously. So I was right, wasn't I? About your story?

**SONJA**     Is that important to you? That you were right?

**DANIEL**     Well, with a woman, it's not very often I get to be right. In fact, usually I just assume that the woman is right. It's so much easier that way. So yes, it is important.

SONJA      Fine. You were right.

DANIEL     You're not a single mother?

SONJA      No.

DANIEL     And you have money?

SONJA      I have a good job and I make an average wage, but every once in a while I like to pamper myself.

DANIEL     Hence the boots.

SONJA      And the gorgeous hair. You forgot the gorgeous hair.

DANIEL     Right. It looks good.

SONJA      You think so?

DANIEL     Very nice.

SONJA      Because I wasn't sure about the colour. I've never had it this colour before.

DANIEL     Oh no, it's very becoming. It highlights your cheekbones.

SONJA      Oh, thank you.

DANIEL     So, what's your job?

SONJA      Hmm?

DANIEL     Your job. What do you do?

SONJA      Oh, we're finished with the hair and the cheekbones already?

DANIEL     I thought it was time to move on, yes.

SONJA      I see. Well, I'm a dermatologist.

DANIEL     Skin doctor.

SONJA      Correct.

DANIEL     Hmm.

SONJA      What's wrong?

DANIEL     Well, you said you make an average wage. I thought a skin doctor would make good money.

SONJA      Well, yeah, in season.

DANIEL     In season? There's a skin season?

SONJA      Of course there's a skin season. Summer.

DANIEL     Why summer?

SONJA      Because of the sun. You know, ultraviolet rays?

DANIEL     Hmm. A skin season. I didn't know that.

SONJA   Well, you're not a dermatologist.

DANIEL   No, I'm not.

SONJA   What are you?

DANIEL   Excuse me?

SONJA   What do you do?

DANIEL   Oh. I'm a counsellor at senior's home. I advise families of the residents about care-giving and planning. I also do some grief counselling. You know, anything to make the golden years of our older generation a little more comfortable.

SONJA   Oh. That's very altruistic of you.

DANIEL   Well, we owe that to them I think. We owe them that much at least. In fact, that's why I'm here right now. The nursing staff forgot to get a Christmas tree for the home and Jenny—she's one of our oldest residents— Jenny pointed out to me that there should be a festive tree for the residents to gather round on Christmas morning. She's a real fire plug, that one. She's got the constitution of a forty-year-old, I swear. So I told her that I would go out immediately and get a tree. It brought a smile to her face, I can tell you that much. That's the real paycheque for me. The smiles. Oh, sure I get a salary but the wages I take home with me are the smiles. Of course I had no idea that this would be the last tree in the entire city, and that someone else would be wanting it too. I'm going to hate to see those time-worn smiles turn to disappointment.

SONJA   So, which home?

DANIEL   I'm sorry?

SONJA   Which senior's home?

DANIEL   Oh, uh…St. Elmo's.

SONJA   St. Elmo's?

DANIEL   St. Elmo's. A little due west of here. *(He points.)*

SONJA   That's east.

DANIEL   East of here. Right. I got turned around I guess.

SONJA   I didn't know there was a St. Elmo.

DANIEL   You know neither did I, until I started working there. But apparently he's the patron saint of seniors.

SONJA   Really?

DANIEL   Yep.

SONJA   So seniors have a saint, do they?

DANIEL   Yeah. Yeah. A Spanish saint from what I understand. Originally he was the patron saint of senors and over time that morphed into seniors.

| | |
|---|---|
| SONJA | The patron saint of senors. |
| DANIEL | That's right. |
| SONJA | You're not a counsellor at all, are you? |
| DANIEL | No, I'm not. And you're not a dermatologist. |
| SONJA | No, I'm not. |
| DANIEL | I figured. Skin season. |
| SONJA | It was better than St. Elmo. |
| DANIEL | Well, you caught me off guard. I had to think fast. |
| SONJA | That whole Jenny thing was a nice touch though. |
| DANIEL | Thank you. |
| SONJA | So, what are you really doing here on Christmas Eve? |
| DANIEL | Well… |
| SONJA | And I mean the real reason. |
| DANIEL | …All right, I'll tell you. |
| SONJA | Wait a minute. I have to sit. |
| DANIEL | Ah! You see? Storytelling is a sitting thing. |
| SONJA | No, it's not that. My feet hurt. Stupid boots are too tight. |

*SONJA sits.*

| | |
|---|---|
| DANIEL | They look good though. |
| SONJA | That's the main thing. All right, lay it on me. |
| DANIEL | All right. I was at the gym tonight and I ran into this friend of mine who's a lumber salesman. Well, lumber sales are slow right now because it's winter and nobody's building decks, right? Nobody's building sheds. Nobody's building gazebos. Anyway, he was bemoaning the fact that he couldn't afford a Christmas tree for the family this year. And he didn't know how to tell his kids. He didn't want to look like a failure in their eyes, you know? So, he told them the tree was on backorder. He told them it was in a warehouse in Duluth. |
| SONJA | Why Duluth? |
| DANIEL | Well, it's so much easier to blame the Americans. But it's ironic, isn't it? A lumber salesman can't afford a tree. Ironic and sad all at once. |
| SONJA | It's unbelievable. |
| DANIEL | I know. |
| SONJA | No, I mean I don't believe it. |
| DANIEL | Why not? |

SONJA     I don't believe you go to a gym.

DANIEL     You what? How can you not believe that? Look at me. I'm in the best shape of my... all right here's the real story. The absolute truth.

SONJA     How do I know that?

DANIEL     What?

SONJA     Well, you've lied to me twice. How do I know you won't do it a third time?

DANIEL     Because this story is the reason I lied to you twice. I've been trying to avoid telling you this story—the true story—because it makes me look like a loser.

SONJA     Why would you care about looking like a loser to me? I don't even know you.

DANIEL     Yeah, but you're a woman.

SONJA     So?

DANIEL     So maybe there's a chance that we'll...you know?

SONJA     That we'll what?

DANIEL     You know? Hook up.

SONJA     Hook up? You and me?

DANIEL     Sure.

SONJA     Why on earth would you think that?

DANIEL     Men always think that. That's what keeps us going. That's what gets us through the day. If we meet an attractive woman, we always think there's a chance that we'll hook up with you.

SONJA     Really?

DANIEL     Always.

SONJA     No, I meant you really think I'm attractive?

DANIEL     Sure.

SONJA     Oh.

DANIEL     You don't think you are?

SONJA     Well, I used to think so.

DANIEL     And what happened to make you stop?

SONJA     I don't know. I guess my confidence got shaken.

DANIEL     So, you have low self-esteem?

SONJA     I guess maybe I do.

DANIEL    Excellent.

SONJA    Why is that excellent?

DANIEL    Well, that puts you one step closer to hooking up with someone like me.

SONJA    Sounds like you have low self-esteem too.

DANIEL    No, I think my self-esteem is right on the money.

SONJA    Are you going to tell me the story now?

DANIEL    What story?

SONJA    You know? The absolute truth?

DANIEL    Oh right. Okay, here it is. And promise me you won't think less of me after you hear this.

SONJA    Impossible.

DANIEL    Good. All right. I've been seeing this woman for the past six months. Susan. And things were going really well, you know? I thought this might be the one. The relationship that was finally going to stick. I mean, Susan is bright, funny, attractive, and she's smart.

SONJA    I guess opposites do attract.

DANIEL    ...Right. Anyway, we had planned to spend Christmas at her place—it was going to be our first Christmas together. Kind of a watershed in the relationship—and so I didn't bother buying a Christmas tree for my place. What would be the point, right? We weren't even going to be there. And look at the money I saved.

SONJA    So you're cheap.

DANIEL    No, I'm not cheap. I'm just not a spendthrift.

SONJA    That's cheap.

DANIEL    Do you want to hear the story or not?

SONJA    Please. Continue.

DANIEL    So last night we were at her apartment. I made dinner for us because I like to cook.

SONJA    What'd ya make?

DANIEL    Linguini. A garlic salmon linguini. So we had just finished dinner and we were tasting a nice white wine that I'd purchased...

SONJA    White wine with pasta?

DANIEL    The white wine works better with the salmon. Besides, pasta is quite flexible where wine is concerned.

SONJA    Really?

**DANIEL**  Oh, it's very forgiving. So we were just settling into the Riesling, when we had this falling out. A huge disagreement. Huge.

**SONJA**  What about?

**DANIEL**  What about?

**SONJA**  Yes. What was the disagreement about?

**DANIEL**  It doesn't matter. It's not germane to the story.

**SONJA**  I'd like to know anyway.

**DANIEL**  Why?

**SONJA**  Because I like to know the details.

**DANIEL**  You're trying to trip me up again, aren't you?

**SONJA**  If you're telling the truth I won't be able to trip you up.

**DANIEL**  That's right.

**SONJA**  You'll have nothing to worry about.

**DANIEL**  I don't.

**SONJA**  So tell me what the disagreement was about.

**DANIEL**  All right, but it's really not important. It's superfluous.

**SONJA**  Wow. Nice word.

**DANIEL**  Thank you.

**SONJA**  I'll have to write that one down later on.

**DANIEL**  You're being sarcastic.

**SONJA**  Yes, I am. Now, what was the disagreement about?

**DANIEL**  Well, she got a job offer in Australia and she took it. She didn't even consult me about it. She just accepted it. And now she expects me to move there with her. Well what am I going to do in Australia? Hang out with the Kiwis? I don't even speak Kiwi.

**SONJA**  Kiwis are in New Zealand.

**DANIEL**  I know. I know that. But I'm sure there are some Kiwis in Australia too. I'm sure they just come and go across that bridge all the time.

**SONJA**  New Zealand and Australia are a thousand miles apart. There is no bridge.

**DANIEL**  ...May I continue?

**SONJA**  Go right ahead.

**DANIEL**  Thank you.

**SONJA**  And they speak English.

**DANIEL**   Who does?

**SONJA**   The Kiwis.

**DANIEL**   All right, so my *National Geographic* subscription has lapsed, okay? Anyway, I told Suzanne that I wasn't moving to Australia with her and we had this big argument and she asked me to leave. She said we were through. So I went back to my undecorated apartment and I decided that if I was going to spend Christmas alone I should at least have a tree, and so here I am.

**SONJA**   Susan.

**DANIEL**   Hmm?

**SONJA**   Her name was Susan. At least it was when you started the story.

**DANIEL**   And when I finished it?

**SONJA**   Suzanne.

**DANIEL**   Darn it.

**SONJA**   So, you lied to me again.

**DANIEL**   Yes, I did. Yes. And by the way, I thought the "opposites do attract" comment was uncalled for.

**SONJA**   But the woman doesn't even exist. So the comment is moot.

**DANIEL**   But, if she did exist, then it would have been completely uncalled for.

**SONJA**   Fine. If she did exist, I would apologize.

**DANIEL**   Apology accepted. If she existed.

**SONJA**   *(looks at her watch)* It's almost eight o'clock, you know. The lot's going to close soon. We have to settle this.

**DANIEL**   All right, so, what's your real story? Why are you here on Christmas Eve?

**SONJA**   Me?

**DANIEL**   Yeah, your turn. Here, let me sit now. You tell me a story.

*DANIEL sits. SONJA stands.*

**SONJA**   You really want to hear my story?

**DANIEL**   Absolutely.

**SONJA**   You've got no place to be, do you?

**DANIEL**   Pardon me?

**SONJA**   Earlier you told me you had places to be. People to spend the yuletide with. You don't, do you?

**DANIEL**     ...No, I don't. Does that make me a loser?

**SONJA**     Well, not that one thing on it's own, no. Besides, maybe your friends are all out of town. Are they?

**DANIEL**     Sure. Let's go with that. So because I'm alone and I've got no place to be, I'd like you to tell me a story. Go ahead.

**SONJA**     All right. You asked for it.

**DANIEL**     And this is gonna be the truth, right?

**SONJA**     Yes.

**DANIEL**     Good. Hit me.

**SONJA**     I'm a flight attendant. Five hours ago we left Montreal for Denver, but Denver is socked in with a snowstorm so we had to put down here. We've been told that we'll be staying overnight. There are five of us. The pilot, his co-pilot, and three attendants. The pilots are both married with families, and one of the attendants is engaged. They were really counting on being home for Christmas, especially Captain Pollock because he's got a new baby at home. Baby's first Christmas is a very special time for a parent. But now we're stuck here. I just thought it might be nice to have a Christmas tree for them, that's all. I was going to surprise them with it.

**DANIEL**     ...That's it?

**SONJA**     That's it.

**DANIEL**     Well, that's not much of a story.

**SONJA**     I know.

**DANIEL**     There's no illness, injury, suffering.

**SONJA**     The truth is kind of boring, isn't it?

**DANIEL**     It sure is. If it was the truth. But it wasn't.

**SONJA**     What do you mean?

**DANIEL**     I have a brother in Denver. I talked to him on the phone an hour ago. They're not having a snowstorm. In fact, it's beautiful there right now.

**SONJA**     Oh.

**DANIEL**     I can't believe that. You lied to me again?

**SONJA**     Well, you lied to me three times! I was just trying to catch up.

**DANIEL**     You know, you would think that on Christmas Eve—Christmas Eve, no less—you would think that on this holiest of evenings, that a person would be a little more honest. That they wouldn't lie just to deprive a fellow human being of a Christmas tree. I find that a little disturbing, I must say. I can't believe that.

**SONJA**     I can't believe you have a brother in Denver.

DANIEL    I don't.

SONJA    Ohhh! What?

DANIEL    Sorry.

SONJA    Really?

DANIEL    Really.

SONJA    Oh, boy. And I fell for that?

DANIEL    Not bad, huh? Yeah, I'm pretty proud of that one.

SONJA    All right, look, I've got to meet some people in a few minutes. We've got to decide who gets this tree.

DANIEL    Okay, let me tell you the truth. Let me tell you why I need this tree.

SONJA    Again?

DANIEL    Yes.

SONJA    Do you honestly think I'm going to believe you after you've already lied to me three times?

DANIEL    Four times.

SONJA    Four? I thought it was three.

DANIEL    No, four. I've never dated a woman with high-class tastes. In fact, I gravitate towards women who have no taste whatsoever.

SONJA    Or they gravitate towards you.

DANIEL    Once again, uncalled for. So, can I tell you the reason why I need this tree?

SONJA    The real reason?

DANIEL    The real reason. The truth. Finally. Are you ready?

SONJA    For the truth? From a man? I'm always ready for that.

DANIEL    All right, here it is. I have this friend who's a circus clown and last week he got arrested for driving under the influence. I guess somebody slipped some apple schnapps into his seltzer bottle and he got sauced and went for a joy ride in his little clown car. The police pulled him over and said his car wasn't street legal. He said that was because he drove it through a car wash and it shrunk. They asked him where he was going and he said it was the Christmas season and he was going to go a'wassiling, but he couldn't find anyone to wassil with so he was just going to go home and watch the Yule Log channel. So anyway, they released him into my care and he's staying at my house over Christmas. I said we should get a Christmas tree but he said he could make one out of balloons. Well, last night he did, but every time we tried to hang an ornament on it we'd burst a balloon. And that's why I'm here on Christmas Eve.

*SONJA stares at him for a beat, then breaks into laughter.*

What's wrong?

*DANIEL starts to laugh too.*

Yeah it wasn't very good, was it?

| | |
|---|---|
| SONJA | No, it was very good. It was exceptional. |
| DANIEL | But you didn't believe it. |
| SONJA | No, I didn't. |
| DANIEL | What gave it away? The car wash? The apple schnapps? |
| SONJA | *(She is still laughing.)* I didn't believe any of it. But thank you. |
| DANIEL | For what? |
| SONJA | For making me laugh. I thought I'd forgotten how. |
| DANIEL | Oh. Bad day? |
| SONJA | Day? Yeah. Bad day all right. |
| DANIEL | Me too. This is the worst time of year to be having a rough go of it. The bad gets magnified this time of year. We tend to wallow in self-pity because there are so many joyful people out there right now. Everywhere you turn people are smiling and saying "Merry Christmas." |
| SONJA | It's annoying, isn't it? |
| DANIEL | No, not really. I like the glad tidings. It gives me hope. Besides, this time of year things probably seem worse to us than they really are anyway. |
| SONJA | Maybe. |
| DANIEL | Oh no, I'm sure that's what it is. |
| SONJA | ...I remember when I was a kid, how wonderful Christmas used to be. The days leading up to it I felt as though I was going burst with excitement. And then Christmas Eve would come and I'd be with my family and everyone was in such a good mood. So happy. I felt like I was wrapped up in the arms of these beautiful people that I loved so much, and I knew that they loved me and I had no idea that one day it wouldn't be like that anymore. That one day they wouldn't be around for me. And I'd be the grown-up and Christmas wouldn't mean to me what it once did. |
| DANIEL | Nothing's the same in the grown-up world. That's the problem with growing up. We leave innocence behind, and the innocence is what made being a kid so much fun. |
| SONJA | Do you think they were that good? Those Christmases? Do you think our parents were really that happy? Or were they as stressed out and jaded as we are now? |
| DANIEL | The truth? |

SONJA     If you think you can muster it.

DANIEL    The truth is, I think our parents were every bit as happy and as loving at Christmastime as they appeared to be. And I think the Christmases that we had as kids were every bit as wonderful as we remember them.

SONJA     Do you think so?

DANIEL    I would hate to think otherwise.

SONJA     Yeah. That's why I'm here, you know?

DANIEL    Why?

SONJA     I'm trying to get that feeling back. That feeling I had when I was a ten-year-old girl and I didn't have a care in the world. And Christmas Eve found me with my little hands holding a cup of hot cocoa, and with my father sitting in his big easy chair watching *A Christmas Carol*, and with my mother pushing the hair away from my face and telling me I'd better go to bed so Santa Claus could come. And he always did. Santa Claus always came. I thought if I got a Christmas tree, it might help me forget that I'm alone this year. That's what I didn't want to tell you. That I'm alone. I didn't want to appear any more wretched than I actually am. Even to a stranger.

DANIEL    You probably thought the same thing I did.

SONJA     And what's that?

DANIEL    That we were going to hook up.

SONJA     No, I didn't think that. No.

DANIEL    Are you sure?

SONJA     Yes! Women don't think that.

DANIEL    No?

SONJA     No.

DANIEL    Well, what do women think? I mean, when they meet a guy for the first time like you're meeting me, what do they think?

SONJA     They think: "I hope he doesn't hit on me because I hate being hit on, but if he does hit on me I hope gives me a couple days to get ready for the date because that's how long it takes these days, and isn't there a sports bar that this gomer should be sitting in with his high-fiving, beer-swilling friends, and why didn't he notice my new coat that I paid two hundred dollars for and which fits me like a glove, and do some men actually still wear Old Spice, and why did I pick today of all days to go out of the house without any makeup on, and how long before this doofus cheats on me and I have to scratch his eyes out?"

DANIEL    ...Yeah, I'm starting to get the picture now. All right, look, why don't you uh... why don't you just take the tree?

SONJA     Really?

DANIEL    Sure. You grabbed it first. Go ahead.

SONJA    You're serious? You're going to let me take the tree?

DANIEL    Sure, what the heck.

SONJA    Oh. All right. Well, thank you.

DANIEL    No problem.

SONJA    That's very kind of you.

DANIEL    Sure.

SONJA    I didn't scare you, did I?

DANIEL    Maybe just a bit.

SONJA    Sorry.

DANIEL    Forget it. Well, I guess I'd better get going. Maybe it's not too late to find another tree somewhere.

> *DANIEL begins to leave.*

See you later.

SONJA    Wait.

> *DANIEL stops.*

Are you letting me have this tree because you think my life is more pathetic than yours?

DANIEL    No, I just...

SONJA    Because it's not. It's not more pathetic. I'm sure your life is way more pathetic than mine.

DANIEL    I'm sure it is.

SONJA    Good. Just so long as you understand that.

DANIEL    Wait a minute. Isn't that what we were trying to do? To prove that our own life was the more pathetic life so that we could have the tree?

SONJA    Yes, but we were telling lies. We were making up those lousy lives. I don't want you to think that my life is really more pathetic than yours.

DANIEL    Listen, I'm sure my life is the far more pathetic life.

SONJA    You think so?

DANIEL    I'm positive. My life is appalling. It's abysmal.

SONJA    Good.

DANIEL    Feel better now?

SONJA    Much.

DANIEL    Great. Enjoy the tree.

*DANIEL starts to leave again.*

| | |
|---|---|
| SONJA | Wait. |
| DANIEL | What?! |
| SONJA | What if you don't find a tree? |
| DANIEL | Then it will be the perfect end to a perfect evening. |
| SONJA | No, really. I'm serious. What if you don't find one? |
| DANIEL | It's all right. Don't worry about it. |
| SONJA | Wait a minute. Come on. I mean, I'm not completely uncharitable. I would like to think that I can have some compassion at this time of year. That I have a heart. |
| DANIEL | So what are you saying? Are you worried about me now? |
| SONJA | No, I'm not worried about you. |
| DANIEL | Then you've got a guilty conscience. |
| SONJA | No, I don't have a guilty conscience. |
| DANIEL | Then you feel sorry for me. |
| SONJA | Well, that goes without saying. |
| DANIEL | I meant because I have no tree! |
| SONJA | Look, I just don't think it would be fair if I had a Christmas tree and you didn't, that's all. |
| DANIEL | So you want to give me the tree now? |
| SONJA | No. After all I went through to get it? No. I just think there must be some way that we can work this out. |
| DANIEL | It's okay. Really. I'll drive around for a while and see if I can find a tree, and if I can't I'll just go home and decorate my dog. It's no big deal. Okay? So, enjoy your tree. Enjoy your Christmas. Feliz Navidad. |

*DANIEL begins to leave.*

| | |
|---|---|
| SONJA | I'll share it with you. |
| DANIEL | I beg your pardon. |
| SONJA | I'll share the tree with you. |
| DANIEL | What do mean share it? How are we gonna share it? Where? |
| SONJA | Right here. We'll buy the tree, take it out to the parking lot, and spend a couple of hours with it out there. |
| DANIEL | What? |
| SONJA | Sure. It's not that cold. We can last a couple of hours out there. |

**DANIEL**    Doing what?

**SONJA**    I don't know. Sitting around the tree. I've got a couple of folding chairs in my trunk.

**DANIEL**    I thought you had to meet some people in a few minutes.

**SONJA**    Well, I do, but they can wait. Two hours won't matter.

**DANIEL**    You're not meeting anyone, are you?

**SONJA**    Of course I am. A couple of friends from work.

**DANIEL**    Hey. You just told me a couple of minutes ago that you were alone. Remember? Or was that a lie too?

**SONJA**    ...No, that was the truth. I'm not meeting anyone. There are no friends.

**DANIEL**    Boy, we're quite the pair, aren't we?

**SONJA**    Yeah.

**DANIEL**    And you want to spend Christmas Eve sitting in a parking lot with me?

**SONJA**    Well, any port in a storm.

**DANIEL**    Oh yeah, that's what a man likes to hear.

**SONJA**    Do you want to share the tree or not? *(beat)* All right, look, forget it then. It was probably a dumb idea. You're right. We don't even know each other. Why would we want to spend Christmas Eve together? *(She grabs hold of the tree.)* I'll just haul the stupid tree home and put the stupid decorations on it myself. Yeah, merry freakin' Christmas.

**DANIEL**    There's a coffee shop across the street.

**SONJA**    What?

**DANIEL**    A coffee shop. They've probably got some hot cocoa. We could get some to go. What d'ya think?

**SONJA**    ...Sure. We could do that.

**DANIEL**    Good.

**SONJA**    And I've got a Christmas CD in my car.

**DANIEL**    Really?

**SONJA**    Yeah.

**DANIEL**    You drive around all depressed on Christmas Eve and you listen to Christmas music? That's sick.

**SONJA**    I like Christmas music.

**DANIEL**    What's you favourite carol?

SONJA     Come on. "Joy to the World."

DANIEL    "The First Noel."

SONJA     Well, it's not bad but it's no "Joy to the World." Now grab an end and let's go.

DANIEL    You know what this means, don't you?

SONJA     What?

DANIEL    We're hooking up.

SONJA     No, we're not.

DANIEL    Yes, we are.

SONJA     We are not.

DANIEL    Oh I think we are. You see? I was right. It is possible.

SONJA     We're not hooking up. We're having cocoa in a parking lot.

DANIEL    That's more than I've done on some dates.

SONJA     This is not a date. It's a chance encounter.

DANIEL    Yeah, well you take it where you can get it.

SONJA     Yeah, that's what a woman likes to hear. Now grab an end, will ya?

DANIEL    You know, I don't know anything about you.

SONJA     So? I don't know anything about you either.

DANIEL    I know. We've been lying to each other since the moment we met. That's not a good way to begin a relationship.

SONJA     This is not a relationship.

DANIEL    It could be.

SONJA     No, it couldn't.

DANIEL    It might be.

SONJA     No, it mightn't. Now pick up the tree.

          *They pick up the tree.*

DANIEL    Wait.

SONJA     What?

DANIEL    What's your name? At least you can tell me that much.

SONJA     Sonja. What's yours?

DANIEL    Daniel.

SONJA     Well, nice to meet you, Daniel.

DANIEL    Nice to meet you, Sonja. Is that your real name?

**SONJA**    No.

*They begin to exit with the tree.*

**DANIEL**    Me neither.

*They exit with the Christmas tree. Lights down.*

*End.*

# Bob's Your Elf

*Bob's Your Elf* was first produced at the Upper Canada Playhouse in Morrisburg, Ontario, with the following cast production team:

| | |
|---|---|
| BOB | Richard Bauer |
| SANTA CLAUS/HOWARD | Doug Tangey* |
| LES BANTER | Tim Hughes |
| GORD FORD | Garfield Andrews |
| FIONA PUTZLE | Linda Goranson |
| AMBER FAIRCASTLE | Liz Gilroy |

* The roles of SANTA Claus and HOWARD must be doubled.

Director: Donnie Bowes
Stage manager: Jackie McCormick
Set designer: John Thompson
Lighting designer: Michael Groenenberg
Costume designer: Alex Amini
Assistant stage manager: Sandi Becker

## ACT ONE Scene One

*Time: The present.*

*Place: SANTA's office.*

*SANTA Claus and BOB the Elf enter. SANTA is dressed in the traditional SANTA costume. Red suit, black boots, etc.... BOB is dressed in a cool outfit. Not the traditional green elf outfit with the striped stockings and curly toed shoes. He wears a longer coat and a stylish cap and cool shoes. Maybe sneakers or funky boots.*

**SANTA**    Come right in, Bob. This won't take but a moment. Can I get you anything? Hot chocolate? Blueberry muffin? Fruit Roll-Up?

**BOB**    No thanks.

**SANTA**    Oatmeal raisin cookie? Black forest cake?

**BOB**    No thanks S., I'm good.

**SANTA**    Mrs. Claus made some double-fudge brownies this morning. I could offer you one of... no, wait. I finished those off already.

**BOB**    I'm fine, Santa.

**SANTA**    Maybe some Twinkies. No, that was brunch.

**BOB**    Santa, I'm good. Really. I can't stay long anyway. I've gotta bounce. I've gotta get back to work. So, what's up? What's the four-one-one?

**SANTA**    Well, Bob, I'd like to talk to you about your future here.

**BOB**    What about my future here?

**SANTA**    Well, I know you're upset because you got passed over for the position of Captain of the Elves.

**BOB**    Gee, do ya think?

**SANTA**    Well, the fact is, I thought that Dewey was better suited for the job.

**BOB**    Oh come on, Santa, I earned that position. And I've got seniority over Dewey. I've been here for a hundred and forty-five years.

**SANTA**    Well, Dewey has been here for a hundred and thirty-two.

**BOB**    Exactly. He's a kid. Plus, Dewey's a Dink.

**SANTA**    I know he's a Dink. I knew his parents. Dickie and Debbie Dink. Wonderful people. Yes, Dewey comes from a long line of Dinks.

**BOB**    Well, we've never had a Dink as Captain of the Elves before.

**SANTA**    No, we haven't.

**BOB**    We've had a Tool.

SANTA        Thomas.

BOB          And a Weiner.

SANTA        Wally.

BOB          But never a Dink.

SANTA        Well, there's a first time for every Dink. And I think Dewey will make a wonderful leader. Even if he is a Dink.

BOB          But he's such a big Dink.

SANTA        Six foot two I believe. Very tall.

BOB          And the clothes he wears. Get real. That bright orange coat? He looks like a traffic pylon.

SANTA        I think he's stylin', Bob.

BOB          Oh, right. And you would know. You've got one colour in your wardrobe. Red.

SANTA        Well, I think Dewey looks fine.

BOB          So, what, you made him captain because you like the way he dresses? Is that why I didn't get the job?

SANTA        No, it goes a lot deeper than that, Bob. And that's what I wanted to talk to you about. The fact is, I've been noticing an attitude problem with you lately.

BOB          Attitude? Dude.

SANTA        I'm serious Bob. I've been watching you and I think you're becoming a bad influence on the rest of the elves.

BOB          What?

SANTA        It's true. You complain all the time, you never smile.

BOB          I didn't know smiling was part of the job.

SANTA        Oh, it is very much a part of the job. The North Pole is a happy place, Bob. We smile, we laugh, we sing. Sometimes we dance.

             *SANTA dances a step or two.*

BOB          Santa? Santa, don't do that, okay? You're scaring me.

SANTA        You don't like my dancing?

BOB          No, that's not dancing, Santa. Trust me. That's more like *American Bandstand* meets Frankenstein.

SANTA        Oh come on, Bob. Join me!

BOB          No thanks.

SANTA        Salsa, Bob! Salsa!

**BOB**        Santa, I don't wanna dance, okay?

**SANTA**      And that is exactly my point. It's very jolly up here and you don't seem to have embraced that jolly spirit. You're not hip to the be bop shoo op, Bob.

**BOB**        I'm not what?

**SANTA**      You're not with the program.

**BOB**        I'm an elf, Santa, I'm not a Rockette. I'm here to work.

**SANTA**      All work and no play.

**BOB**        Gets the job done a lot faster.

**SANTA**      But it doesn't make for a happy workshop.

**BOB**        Work isn't supposed to be fun, Santa. That's why it's called work.

**SANTA**      If you like what you're doing, then work can be a lot of fun. And that brings us back to your attitude. You're not really a team player, are you Bob?

**BOB**        What do you mean?

**SANTA**      I mean, we're a team here. We pull together. We work as one to complete the huge task at hand.

**BOB**        Making the toys.

**SANTA**      Exactly. Making the toys. For the girls and boys. I like that. I'm going to have that put on a T-shirt. Do you think I'd look good in a tee, Bob?

**BOB**        A tee? Yeah, that'd show off your figure nicely. Now, you were saying?

**SANTA**      Hmm?

**BOB**        My bad influence?

**SANTA**      Oh, yes. Well, when one of my elves spends a good portion of the work day complaining, well, it's counterproductive. It's bad for morale. You're bringin' us down, Bob. You're bummin' us out.

**BOB**        S. Come on. I'm the best worker you've got up here. I still hold the North Pole record for the fastest assembly of a cuckoo clock. Thirty-four seconds flat.

**SANTA**      But the clock didn't tock.

**BOB**        Pardon me?

**SANTA**      The clock. It ticked, but it didn't tock. Clock's gotta tock, Bob.

**BOB**        Well, how about my record for the assembly of a rocking horse?

SANTA     But the horse didn't rock. Rocking horse has gotta rock, Bob. Otherwise it's just a sitting-there horse.

BOB     I don't suppose I should bring up the talking sock.

SANTA     Sock didn't talk, Bob. Sock didn't talk.

BOB     Darn it.

SANTA     Bob, look, no one is questioning your talent. I know you're a hard worker. No, it's your behaviour. And that's why I'm sending you away.

BOB     What? Wait a minute. You're sending me away?

SANTA     Yes, I've got an assignment for you.

BOB     You're sending me away?

SANTA     Yes. You're going to a small town called Thithelville.

BOB     I'm sorry? Thistleville?

SANTA     No. Thithelville.

BOB     Thistleville.

SANTA     No. Thithelville.

BOB     Thi…

SANTA     Thel.

BOB     Thel.

SANTA     Thithel.

BOB     Thithel.

SANTA     Ville.

BOB     Ville.

SANTA     Thithelville.

BOB     Thithelville.

SANTA     Right.

BOB     And why am I going there, Santa? What's the deal here?

SANTA     Well, I want you to help them out with a stage production they're doing.

BOB     Help who out?

SANTA     The Thithelville Thespians.

BOB     You don't thay.

SANTA     It's the local theatre group and every year they put on a Christmas pageant for the townspeople. Well, this year they're having some problems and I want you to give them some assistance.

BOB        What kind of problems?

SANTA      You'll find out when you get there.

BOB        How long will I be there? When do I get to come back? Will I be back in time for Christmas?

SANTA      Well, Bob, that depends on what you learn in Thithelville.

BOB        What are you thaying? Saying! I mean, am I going to come back to the North Pole at all? Are you sending me away for good?

SANTA      Let's just wait and see what happens in Thithelville, shall we? Now, I have to get over to the stable. Rudolf left his nose on all night and I've got to change his bulb.

BOB        Don't you have people who do that for you?

SANTA      No, Bob. Now this is exactly what I'm trying to tell you. We all carry an equal share of the load here. No one person is bigger than our mission.

BOB        Making the toys.

SANTA      For the girls and boys. Yes, I do like that. Maybe I could put it on a bumper sticker.

BOB        So when do I leave?

SANTA      Immediately. I've got a sleigh waiting outside for you. I want you in Thithelville for this evening's rehearsal.

BOB        But don't I get a chance to say goodbye to my friends?

SANTA      And who would that be?

BOB        Well.... Prancer and I are buds.

SANTA      He's just being polite, Bob.

BOB        He is?

SANTA      Trust me.

BOB        Oh man.

SANTA      All right. Off we go.

BOB        But I've got to pack first. You know, a toothbrush, socks, some notions.

SANTA      Your bag's already packed. It's in the sleigh.

BOB        Who packed it?

SANTA      Dewey.

BOB        The big Dink.

SANTA      The very same.

*SANTA sings the first verse of "Sleigh Ride."*

*SANTA and BOB exit.*

*End Act One, Scene One.*

## ACT ONE Scene Two

*Time: That evening.*

*Place: The rehearsal hall of the Thithelville Thespians.*

*There are a few chairs in the hall and a table with some donuts. There is also a cradle. The backdrop is a painting of a stable used for the Nativity. There is a door painted on the wall. There is also a small functional window in the wall. BOB and LES Banter enter. LES carries a clipboard and is wearing a set of headphones.*

LES        We're on a ten-minute break right now, but the director should be along momentarily. Why don't you just take a seat off to the side there for the time being? Would that be all right?

BOB        Yeah, that's cool.

LES        *(removing his headphones so he can hear)* What's that?

BOB        I said it's cool.

*BOB moves to a chair at the side of the stage and sits.*

LES        Oh, good. *(puts his headphones back on)* I'm Les by the way. Les Banter. I'm the stage manager. Yes, I pretty much run the show here. No one makes a move without my say-so. I'm the straw that stirs the drink. The pan that fries the egg. The belt that holds up the trousers. The rock in the rock n' roll. Yep, a lot of people think it's the director who's the boss, but believe me, that's a complete falsehood. It's poppycock. Puffin stuff. Twaddle. No, I'm the top dog in this kennel, my friend.

*GORD Ford enters. He carries a script.*

GORD        All right everyone! Could I have the actors onstage please? The cast. The company. Come out, come out, wherever you are.

LES        Gord?

GORD        Yes?

LES        Gord?

GORD        Yes?

LES        Gord?

GORD        Yes!!?

**LES**    *(He pulls the headphones off of one ear so he can hear.)* The break's over. Would you like me to call for the actors?

**GORD**    I just called for the actors.

**LES**    You did?

**GORD**    Yes.

**LES**    Good.

**GORD**    And by the way, I heard that "top dog" comment.

**LES**    Just shooting my mouth off, Gord. Won't happen again. Actors onstage please! Let's go everyone! Thank you!

> *LES exits. FIONA Putzle enters. She is around sixty years old. She carries a script.*

**FIONA**    I'm sorry. Is the break over already?

**GORD**    It's been over for three minutes, Fiona.

**FIONA**    Oh. Then I'm late?

**GORD**    Ah! I see you've put two and two together at last. Excellent.

**FIONA**    Well, Gordon, I was in my dressing room reading over the script.

**GORD**    Oh, don't jump into that too quickly, Fiona. I mean we open tomorrow night. If you learn your lines too soon you'll throw the rest of the cast into a tizzy.

**FIONA**    Don't worry, my dear. I shan't peak too soon.

**GORD**    I'm sure you shan't.

**FIONA**    Anyway, I was looking at the native scene.

**GORD**    The what?

**FIONA**    The native scene? The birth of the baby?

**GORD**    It's the Nativity scene, Fiona. Not the native scene. Nativity.

**FIONA**    Yes, anyway, I think I should be playing the woman named Mary.

**GORD**    The woman named Mary?

**FIONA**    Yes.

**GORD**    You mean the Virgin Mary?

**FIONA**    If you say so.

**GORD**    Fiona, do you know how old Mary was when she gave birth to our Lord and Saviour?

**FIONA**    No.

**GORD**    Well, she was quite young, my love.

**FIONA**    Yes?

**GORD**    Very young.

**FIONA**    Yes?

**GORD**    And she looked young.

**FIONA**    Yes?

**GORD**    It's.... Never mind. It's a little late to start changing roles now, darling. Besides, we already have a Mary. Amber is playing Mary. Remember?

**FIONA**    Amber. Yes, the little girl named after a shade of stoplight.

**GORD**    She is the right type for the Virgin, Fiona. Fresh-faced. Innocent. Young. And besides, you are much more suited to the role of the Spirit of Christmas Past... because you've witnessed so many of them first-hand.

**FIONA**    What was that?

**GORD**    Nothing, my sweet. Turn your hearing aid down, love. You're picking up the NORAD broadcasts again.

*LES enters.*

**LES**    Gord?

**GORD**    Yes?

**LES**    Gord?

**GORD**    Yes?

**LES**    Gord?

**GORD**    Yes?!

**LES**    Fiona wanted to have a word with you.

**GORD**    I'm having a word with her right now, Les.

*LES pulls his headset off of one ear.*

**LES**    What?

**GORD**    I said I'm... why are you wearing those headphones?

**LES**    Why? Because I'm the stage manager. Stage managers always wear headphones.

**GORD**    But you have no one to talk to.

**LES**    Pardon me?

**GORD**    There is no one on the other end of the headphones. You haven't even... where are they plugged in?

**LES**    What's that?

| | |
|---|---|
| **GORD** | The headphones. The wire. Where is it plugged in? Is it in your shorts? |
| **LES** | Yes. |
| **GORD** | You have your headphones plugged into your underwear? |
| **LES** | Yes. |
| **GORD** | Why? |
| **LES** | Well, they've got to be plugged in somewhere. |
| | *LES exits.* |
| **GORD** | Of course. How foolish of me to ask. |
| | *AMBER Faircastle enters. She is a younger woman. About twenty to thirty years old.* |
| **AMBER** | I'm here! I'm here! Sorry! |
| **GORD** | Ah, and there's our star. Hello, Amber. Welcome back. |
| **AMBER** | I'm sorry I'm late, Gordon. |
| **GORD** | No, think nothing of it. I'm sure I called an end to the break far too soon in fact. My fault entirely. A thousand pardons. |
| **AMBER** | It's just that I was on the phone to my mother. She's not feeling well. |
| **GORD** | Nothing serious I hope. |
| **AMBER** | No, I think she's just lonely now that all of us kids are out of the house. I mean, Colin and Colleen are off to college, Jasmine jumped at a job in Jasper, Timmy's teaching in Timmins, the twins are in Tucson, and Mindy's moved to Minsk. |
| **GORD** | And now your mother's all alone in that shoe. |
| **AMBER** | Yes. |
| **GORD** | Well, don't worry, precious. Your mother's needs come first and I am more than happy to accommodate you in seeing to those needs. |
| **AMBER** | Thank you, Gordon. That's very kind. |
| **GORD** | I know. |
| | *LES enters.* |
| **LES** | Gord? |
| **GORD** | Yes? |
| **LES** | Gord? |
| **GORD** | Yes? |
| **LES** | Gord? |

| GORD | Yes?! |
|---|---|
| LES | *(pulls the headset off of one ear)* Amber's back. |
| GORD | Yes, I know, Les. I'm standing here talking to her. |
| LES | Check. |
| GORD | And where's Howard? |
| LES | Pardon me? |
| GORD | Howard. Our Santa Claus. Where is he? |
| LES | He's trying on his costume. He'll be along shortly. |
| FIONA | Long shortly? How can someone be long and shortly? I don't understand. |
| GORD | It's nothing, Fiona. Have another prune, sweetheart. |
| LES | I'll go and hurry him up. |
| GORD | Yes, do that. Thank you so much. |

     *LES exits.*

| BOB | Yo, yo. |
|---|---|
| GORD | Yes, yes? |
| BOB | Zup? |
| GORD | Zup? Is that what you said? Zup? |
| BOB | Yeah. What's shakin'? |
| GORD | Who are you? What are you doing here? Can I help you? |
| BOB | I'm Bob. I take it you're the director? |
| GORD | Yes. Gordon Ford. What can I do for you? |
| BOB | Uh… well, I'm here to take part I guess. |
| GORD | You guess? |
| BOB | Well, I was sent here to help out. |
| GORD | By who? |
| BOB | My boss. |
| GORD | And that would be? Oh, wait. No, don't tell me. Don't tell me. Mr. Binkins over at Binkins' Grocery. Right? Yes. *(to AMBER)* You see this? You see? You let someone supply you with snacks for the cast—donuts, a couple of limp celery stalks, a cabbage—and all of a sudden they think they're running the show. Well, fine. All right. Our Joseph had to back out at the last minute due to a fear of donkeys, so you can be Joseph. |
| BOB | Joseph who? |

**GORD**    Joseph who? You know, Mary and Joseph? No room at the inn? The parents? Have you met Fiona?

**FIONA**    Hello!

**BOB**    Waz up, boo?

**FIONA**    *(to GORD)* Who's this?

**GORD**    Pardon me?

**FIONA**    Who's this fellow I just said hello to?

**BOB**    My name is Bob.

**FIONA**    Hello, Bob.

**BOB**    Hello.

**FIONA**    *(She shakes BOB's hand.)* Fiona Putzle. Charmed, I'm sure.

**BOB**    Likewise.

**AMBER**    Hello. I'm Amber Faircastle.

**BOB**    *(shaking AMBER's hand)* Hi.

**AMBER**    I'm your wife.

**BOB**    My what?

**AMBER**    I'm playing Mary.

**BOB**    Oh. Right on.

**FIONA**    And I am the Spirit of Christmas Past.

*FIONA does her best witch impersonation.*

Who dropped that house on my sister?! Was it you, little girl?! I'll get you, my pretty. And your little dog too!

**GORD**    Dazzling, Fiona. Unfortunately, that's the Wicked Witch of the West. Not the Spirit of Christmas Past.

**FIONA**    Oh fizzle.

**BOB**    Actually, I was hoping I could be an elf.

**GORD**    I beg your pardon?

**BOB**    An elf. Do you have any elves in the show? Because I think I'd be a slammin' elf.

**GORD**    An elf?

**BOB**    Yes.

**GORD**    You're a little tall for an elf, aren't you? I mean, there's no Andre the Elf as far as I know. No Kareem Abdul the Elf, right?

**BOB**    Who says an elf has to be short?

**GORD**     Well the word alone implies shortness, doesn't it? Elf? He was elfin? Hey, elf, you're pretty short?

**BOB**     Actually, that's a myth.

**GORD**     What ith?

**BOB**     That elves are short. They're not all short.

**GORD**     Really? And how would you know this?

**BOB**     Because I'm an elf.

**GORD**     No, you're Joseph.

**BOB**     No, I mean, I'm a real elf. I'm legit. I'm street legal.

**GORD**     Uh-huh. Well, I think you make a more believable Joseph. 'Kay? Thank you. Thank you ever so—

> *LES and HOWARD enter. HOWARD is wearing a blue SANTA Claus costume.*

**HOWARD**     Gordon? Gordon, I seem to be having a problem with my costume.

**GORD**     And what problem would that be, Howard?

**LES**     Gord?

**GORD**     Yes?

**LES**     Gord?

**GORD**     Yes?

**LES**     Gord?

**GORD**     Yes!?

**LES**     *(pulls the headset off of one ear)* Howard's here.

**GORD**     I know he is, Les. Thank you. *(to HOWARD)* And what problem are you having, Howard?

**HOWARD**     Well, it's a wee bit small.

**GORD**     Small?

**HOWARD**     A wee bit.

**GORD**     How could it be too small? It's a size fifty-two chunky, Howard. It's from the Jabba the Hutt collection.

**HOWARD**     I don't know. I can't explain it. *(looking at the food)* Ooh, is that a fritter? Scrumptious. *(He moves to the food table.)*

**BOB**     It's blue.

**GORD**     I'm sorry?

BOB       His Santa suit. It's blue.

GORD     Yes, it is. And you've passed the colour-blind test. Congratulations.

BOB       But Santa wears a red suit.

AMBER    That's what I said too.

GORD     And how do you know Santa wears a red suit, my dear? Have you seen Santa?

AMBER    Well, no.

GORD     Fiona? Have you seen Santa?

FIONA     Why? Is he missing?

GORD     Never mind.

BOB       I've seen Santa.

GORD     Pardon me?

BOB       I've seen Santa Claus. And he's sportin' a red suit.

GORD     You've seen Santa. Very good. Well, Bob, I'm the director, and I say Santa wears a blue suit. I will not have my Christmas pageant smothered by urban clichés. Howard, come with me. Perhaps the seamstress can let that suit out for you.

HOWARD  Crackerjack idea. Mmmmm… Crackerjacks.

           *HOWARD pulls a box of Crackerjacks out of his suit. HOWARD and LES exit.*

GORD     Fiona?

FIONA     Yes, dear?

GORD     Are you coming?

FIONA     Why would I do that?

GORD     Because you're the seamstress.

FIONA     I am?

GORD     Yes.

FIONA     Then I should probably come along.

GORD     Capital idea.

           *GORD and FIONA exit. AMBER looks at BOB and laughs.*

AMBER    A real elf. That's funny. You're funny, Bob.

BOB       Well, I am a real elf.

AMBER    *(laughing again)* Oh stop.

**BOB**    It's the truth.

**AMBER**    You know, I like a fella with a sense of humour. Laughter is the best medicine, right? You make a person laugh, and you make them feel good all over.

**BOB**    Uh-huh.

**AMBER**    You cure what ails 'em.

**BOB**    Right

**AMBER**    So, here we are. Husband and wife.

**BOB**    What's that?

**AMBER**    You and me. Joseph and Mary. Husband and wife.

**BOB**    Oh, right. Right.

**AMBER**    Yes, it's nice to finally have someone. Now I won't be alone anymore.

**BOB**    What?

**AMBER**    Nothing. Just dreaming out loud.

**BOB**    Oh.

**AMBER**    Yes, it'll be nice to have a friendly face across the dinner table. Someone to talk to. To share a humorous anecdote with. The news of the day. Someone I can go walking with on a moonlit night. You know, when the moon lights up the night and it's all lit? And we'll walk for hours and a strange old man will ask us how to get to Poughkeepsie and we won't know and we won't care because we're so smitten with each other. Yes, someone I can go bowling with and who can help me when my fingers get stuck in those little holes and I can't let go of the ball and I go careening down the alley face first and wind up scoring a seven-ten split. Not that that's ever happened. I usually spare it up.

**BOB**    Are they gonna be long?

**AMBER**    I hope so.

**BOB**    Pardon me?

**AMBER**    How old are you, Bob?

**BOB**    What?

**AMBER**    How old are you, Bob?

**BOB**    How old?

**AMBER**    How old are you, Bob?

**BOB**    Why do you ask?

**AMBER**     Just curious. Because we look about the same age, that's all. We look like we could be a couple. Like Joseph and Mary.

**BOB**     I'm a hundred and seventy-three.

*After a beat, AMBER laughs.*

What's wrong?

**AMBER**     A hundred and seventy-three.

**BOB**     I know. I look a lot younger. People always tell me I don't look a day over a century.

*AMBER laughs and slaps BOB playfully on the shoulder.*

**AMBER**     Stop!

**BOB**     Ow.

**AMBER**     So, tell me about yourself, Bob. Who is Bob? Who is this charming chap with the chiselled chin? I want to know all about him.

**BOB**     Uh... well...

**AMBER**     Myself, I was born in Thithelville. Born and raised. I'm a townie. Uh-huh. I have a variety of interests. I enjoy extreme dominoes, garlic pressing, and long walks on the beach. Of course there is no beach here, but if you walk down by the sewage treatment plant I swear you can almost hear the waves crashing. What do you like, Bob? What's Bob's passion? What does Bob do for F-U-N?

**BOB**     F-U- Oh, fun.... Uh... I don't do anything for fun.

**AMBER**     *Pardon moi*, Bob?

**BOB**     I said I do nothing for fun.

**AMBER**     But, that's impossible. Everybody does something for fun. I mean all work and no play, right?

**BOB**     Well, not me. I just work.

**AMBER**     Hmm. That's very sad, Bob. Extremely sad. Über sad.

**BOB**     Why is that sad?

**AMBER**     A person who gets no fun out of life? That's terribly sad. What about friends? Don't you have friends?

**BOB**     Well, there was one, but it turns out he was just being polite.

**AMBER**     Awwww. I'll be your friend, Bob.

**BOB**     Pardon me?

**AMBER**     I'll be your friend, Bob.

**BOB**     You?

| | |
|---|---|
| **AMBER** | I'll be your friend, Bob. |
| **BOB** | Really? |
| **AMBER** | Sure. And I won't do it because I think you're a poor, poor, pitiful, pathetic poop either. No, I'll do it because I actually like you. |
| **BOB** | You do? |
| **AMBER** | I sure dippity do. |
| **BOB** | Oh. Well, thank you. |
| **AMBER** | No thanks required. It's my pleasure. Yessiree, Bob. |

*GORD, LES, FIONA, and HOWARD enter.*

| | |
|---|---|
| **GORD** | Les, there was no need to lock the wardrobe department door. |
| **LES** | I know, Gord. I'm sorry. |
| **GORD** | And how could you misplace the key? You've got every key in existence on that key chain. |
| **LES** | I don't know. Maybe someone backstage took it. |
| **GORD** | There is no one backstage. |
| **LES** | I'll ask them. Don't worry. I'll get to the bottom of this. |

*LES exits.*

| | |
|---|---|
| **HOWARD** | So I should wear the suit as is, Gordon? |
| **GORD** | Until we have access to wardrobe, Howard, yes. |
| **HOWARD** | All right, but it's beginning to squeeze the very life out of me. *(looking at the donuts)* Mmmm. Boston Cream. *(He moves to the donuts.)* |
| **FIONA** | *(looking through her script)* Gordon, I've lost my place. Where were we? |
| **GORD** | We haven't started yet, love. |
| **FIONA** | We haven't? |
| **GORD** | No. |
| **FIONA** | Well, that's unfortunate. What are we waiting for? |
| **GORD** | Howard's costume is too tight. |
| **FIONA** | Well, you should get the seamstress to let it out for him then. |
| **GORD** | Good thinking, dear. I shall call her first thing. All right, can we begin now please? Everyone ready? |
| **AMBER** | Ready Teddy. |
| **GORD** | Thank you. Wonderful. Let's start from page twelve then, shall we? Ebenezer Scrooge visiting the manger. |

| | |
|---|---|
| **BOB** | What? |
| **GORD** | Ebenezer Scrooge visiting the manger. |
| **FIONA** | Where? |
| **GORD** | Ebenezer Scrooge visiting the manger. |

*LES enters.*

| | |
|---|---|
| **LES** | Gord? |
| **GORD** | Yes? |
| **LES** | Gord? |
| **GORD** | Yes? |
| **LES** | Gord? |
| **GORD** | Yes?! |
| **LES** | *(pulls the headset off of one ear)* Where are we starting from? |
| **GORD** | Page twelve. |
| **LES** | Page twelve, everybody! |
| **BOB** | Ebenezer Scrooge visiting the manger? |
| **GORD** | That's right. Where the baby Jesus waits, wrapped in swaddling clothes. |

*He looks in the cradle.*

Where is he? Where's the baby Jesus?! Anyone? Les?

| | |
|---|---|
| **LES** | *(pulls the headset off of one ear)* Gord? |
| **GORD** | There's no baby. We can't do the manger scene without the baby. |
| **LES** | Why not? |
| **GORD** | Well that's what the manger scene is all about, Les. The baby. The boy child. The only begotten son. It's not about the livestock or the tumbleweeds. It's about the baby. |
| **LES** | I'm on it, Gord. |

*LES exits, calling off as he goes:*

I need the baby Jesus, people!

| | |
|---|---|
| **GORD** | Who's he talking to? There's no one back there. |
| **BOB** | Ebenezer Scrooge visiting the manger? |
| **GORD** | Yes. Why do you keep saying that? |
| **BOB** | Ebenezer Scrooge didn't visit the manger. |
| **AMBER** | That's what I said too. Right, Fiona? |

**FIONA**    Hello! *(looking at BOB)* Ah, a new face. *(She moves to BOB.)* Hello there. And you are?

**BOB**    Bob.

**FIONA**    *(shaking BOB's hand)* Fiona Putzle. Charmed, I'm sure.

**GORD**    Fiona, you've already been introduced.

**FIONA**    We have?

**GORD**    Yes.

**FIONA**    Oh fuzzle. Then I got up for nothing. Oh well. As long as I'm here, let's chew the fat. *(to BOB)* And who are you playing, Boob?

**BOB**    Bob.

**FIONA**    Bob? Is there a Bob in the script?

**BOB**    No, my name is Bob.

**FIONA**    Oh, I'm sorry. And who are you playing, Bob?

**BOB**    Joseph.

**FIONA**    Joseph? *(to the others)* I thought he said his name was Bob.

**AMBER**    No, Fiona, he's playing Joseph.

**FIONA**    Oh! *(doing her Spirit of Christmas Past)* Joseph! I am the Spirit of Christmas Past!

**GORD**    Fiona, you don't say that to Joseph, darling. You say it to Ebenezer Scrooge.

**FIONA**    Oh farfel.

**BOB**    Which brings me back to my original question. Why is Ebenezer Scrooge at the manger?

**AMBER**    That's what I said too.

**GORD**    Yes, thank you for chiming in, Amber. Always on cue. Brilliant. Bob, the fact of the matter is, we couldn't decide which Christmas story to do for this year's pageant, so we've combined all the best stories. The nativity, *A Christmas Carol*, *The Night Before Christmas*, and *Rudolph the Red-Nosed Reindeer*.

**FIONA**    *(doing her Spirit of Christmas Past)* Rudolph! I am the Spirit of...

**GORD**    Thank you, Fiona. Thank you. Perfect.

        *HOWARD approaches, wiping cream filling from his face.*

**HOWARD**    And who's this then? Someone new in the company?

**BOB**    The name's Bob.

**HOWARD**    Bob! How do you do?

*He holds out his hand to shake.*

Howard Widebottom. A pleasure to make your acquaintance. Oh, pardon the cream. Messy things those.

*He licks the cream off of his fingers.*

Mmmm, that tastes like another.

*He moves back to the donuts.*

| | |
|---|---|
| **BOB** | *(to GORD)* You couldn't decide which story to do? |
| **GORD** | Correct. |
| **AMBER** | Nobody in this town can ever agree on anything. |
| **GORD** | Now that's not true, Amber. |
| **AMBER** | Yes, it is. |
| **GORD** | No, it's not. |
| **AMBER** | Yes, it is. |
| **GORD** | No, it's not. |
| **AMBER** | Yes, it is. |
| **GORD** | No, it's not. |
| **AMBER** | Yes, it is. |
| **GORD** | Then on this matter, we shall have to agree to disagree. |
| **AMBER** | That's the problem. That's what I just said. *(to BOB)* Are you from Thithelville, Bob? Because if you are, you'll know what I'm talking about. |
| **BOB** | No, I'm not from here. |
| **AMBER** | Where are you from? |
| **BOB** | North of here. |
| **AMBER** | Oh. Thathkatoon? |
| **BOB** | I'm sorry? Saskatoon? |
| **AMBER** | No, Thathkatoon. |
| **BOB** | Thathkatoon? |
| **AMBER** | Yes, it's two hours north of here. |
| **BOB** | Uh-huh. And what's south of here? |
| **AMBER** | Gwande Pwawie. |
| **BOB** | Grande Prairie? |
| **AMBER** | No. Gwande Pwawie. |

**GORD**    People, please. We open in twenty-four hours. And it would be a comfort to me if we could run through the show just once before the curtain goes up. Huh? What do ya say? Can we do that?

*LES enters carrying a doll wrapped in swaddling clothes.*

**LES**    Heads up! Part the waters! Baby Jesus comin' through! Where do you want him, Gord?

**GORD**    Well, Les, why don't we put the lad in the cradle? I suspect that's where a newborn might wind up.

**LES**    Check.

*LES puts the doll in the cradle.*

**GORD**    All right, Mary and Joseph please take a seat somewhere near the Chosen One. Thank you. I think we are finally ready to begin.

*AMBER and BOB move to the cradle and sit.*

Now, Fiona, you as the Spirit of Christmas Past have just arrived at the manger with Mister Scrooge, played by yours truly.

**FIONA**    And we've only just met, is that correct?

**GORD**    Pardon me?

**FIONA**    Mister Scrooge and myself are strangers, are we?

**GORD**    Well, yes, love I suppose you are.

**FIONA**    Excellent.

**GORD**    *(to HOWARD)* And Howard…

*FIONA grabs GORD's arm.*

**FIONA**    Ebenezer Scrooge! I have always depended on the kindness of strangers!

**GORD**    Super, Fiona. Don't change a thing. Howard, you are standing by offstage as Santa Claus and you will arrive shortly with Rudolph in tow.

**HOWARD**    I'm standing by.

*HOWARD exits.*

**GORD**    Thank you.

**LES**    Gord?

**GORD**    Yes?

**LES**    Gord?

**GORD**    Yes?

**LES**    Gord?

**GORD**    Yes?!

LES        (*pulls the headset off of one ear*) Where do you want me to go?

GORD      …Well, Les, you're not actually in the production. You work from the backstage area.

LES        Uh-huh?

GORD      So a good place for you might be where?

LES        Uhhhhh…

GORD      Not onstage but…

LES        Uhhhh…

GORD      Anyone know the answer? Anybody? Fiona?

FIONA     Pass.

GORD      Amber?

AMBER     Nope.

GORD      Howard?

HOWARD   (*off*) I'm standing by!

GORD      Wonderful.

BOB       How about backstage?

GORD      Correct! Yes! Thank you!

FIONA     Oh, excellent dear boy.

          *FIONA applauds.*

GORD      Have you got that, Les? Backstage.

LES        Check.

          *LES exits, calling off:*

Standby backstage, everyone! Here we go!

GORD      What is he doing? There's no one back there.

BOB       Excuse me?

GORD      Yes? Question?

BOB       What about the three wise men?

GORD      What's that?

BOB       The three wise men. There were three wise men at the manger. Where are they?

GORD      They will be played by four local school children.

BOB       Four?

**GORD**      Yes. The Jamieson quadruplets. Their mother wouldn't let us break up the set.

**BOB**       Well, what's the fourth one carrying?

**GORD**      Carrying?

**BOB**       Well, the three wise men brought gold, frankincense, and myrrh. What's your fourth wise man carrying?

**GORD**      Potatoes.

**BOB**       Potatoes?

**GORD**      Yes. A five-pound sack of potatoes. Very valuable up here.

*HOWARD enters.*

**HOWARD**  Gordon?

**GORD**      Yes, Howard?

**HOWARD**  Will the fourth wise man be bringing sour cream as well?

**GORD**      Sour cream?

**HOWARD**  Yes. For the baked potatoes.

**GORD**      They're not baked potatoes, Howard. They're raw potatoes.

**HOWARD**  Oh.

**GORD**      Yes.

**HOWARD**  But how is the little Messiah supposed to eat raw potatoes? The tot isn't even teething yet. He'll starve.

**FIONA**     Baby Jesus! As God as my witness you will never be hungry again!

**GORD**      No, Fiona. That's Scarlett O'Hara. But you are narrowing it down. Good for you. Howard? Offstage.

**HOWARD**  Right. I'm standing by.

*HOWARD exits.*

**AMBER**   So, what do you do, Bob? For a living?

**BOB**       I'm an el.... I'm in construction.

**AMBER**   Ooh.

**BOB**       And what about you? What do you do here?

**AMBER**   In Thithelville?

**BOB**       Yeth.

**AMBER**   I'm the town librarian.

**GORD**     And one day we're going to get you a library, sweetheart. That's a promise. I've got a book at home that's going to start the ball rolling. Are we ready to do the scene now?

**AMBER**     Ready Freddy.

**GORD**     Splendid.

*LES pokes his head out from backstage.*

**LES**     Gord?

**GORD**     Yes?

**LES**     Gord?

**GORD**     Yes?

**LES**     Gord?

**GORD**     Yes?!

**LES**     *(pulls the headset off of one ear)* We're all set backstage.

**GORD**     I'm tickled.

*LES exits.*

So, to continue, the Spirit of Christmas Past and Ebenezer Scrooge enter. Fiona, will you join me please?

**FIONA**     Happily.

*FIONA takes GORD's hand and they move towards the cradle.*

**GORD**     Thank you. And we slowly, reverently, and ever so humbly approach the manger.

*We hear a doorbell.*

What the...? What was that?

**AMBER**     Sounded like a doorbell.

**FIONA**     I'll get it.

*FIONA goes to the painted door on the set and bangs into it.*

**GORD**     No, Fiona. There's no one... Les? Les?!

*LES enters.*

**LES**     Gord?

**GORD**     Did I just hear a doorbell?

**LES**     Yes, you did.

**GORD**     And why was that?

**LES**     Well, you're approaching the front door of the stable and I thought it might be good to have the sound effect of a doorbell.

| | |
|---|---|
| **GORD** | Uh-huh. Les, it's the year one! Doorbells are still a few years off yet. |
| **LES** | Oh. |
| **GORD** | Yes. |
| **LES** | So I should probably cut the microwave oven then too, huh? |
| **GORD** | Microwave oven? |
| **LES** | To make popcorn for the wise men. |
| **GORD** | Popcorn? |
| **LES** | Well, they've come a long way. They're probably hungry. |
| **GORD** | Cut the microwave. |
| **LES** | Cut it? |
| **GORD** | Cut it. |
| **LES** | Check. Cut the microwave, people! |

*LES exits to the wings.*

| | |
|---|---|
| **GORD** | All right then. So, we approach the manger, slowly, reverently, and ever so humbly. And I begin. Spirit, what child is this? |
| **FIONA** | Are you going to say it like that? |
| **GORD** | I thought I might, yes. |
| **FIONA** | Oh. |
| **GORD** | Is there a problem? |
| **FIONA** | Not at all. |
| **GORD** | You're sure? |
| **FIONA** | I shall trust your judgment. |
| **GORD** | Thank you. |
| **FIONA** | I'm sure it will play eventually. |
| **GORD** | Thank you so much. And again. Spirit, what child is this? |
| **FIONA** | *(looking at her script)* He is the King of Kings, Mr. Scrounge. |
| **GORD** | Scrooge. |
| **FIONA** | What dear? |
| **GORD** | It's not Mr. Scrounge. It's Mr. Scrooge. |
| **FIONA** | *(looking at her script)* Oh, so it is. Sorry. Someone must have drooled on my script. That's happened a lot lately. Shall we try it again? |

**GORD**    No, let's just say a novena and move on. Here we go. And then Mary says...

**AMBER**    So, are you married, Bob?

**GORD**    *(looks at his script)* What? "Are you married, Bob?" Where's that?

**AMBER**    No, I was just asking Bob if he was married.

**GORD**    Amber, we're rehearsing, my darling.

**AMBER**    Oh. I thought you and Fiona were still discussing.

**GORD**    No, we're done.

**AMBER**    Oh.

**GORD**    All squared away.

**AMBER**    Sorry.

**GORD**    Not a problem.

**BOB**    *(to AMBER)* No, I'm not married.

**AMBER**    Oh? How interesting. I'm not married either. Haven't found the right fella yet. I think they're frightened off because I'm a woman in a position of power.

**BOB**    You're a librarian.

**AMBER**    Yes.

**BOB**    With no library.

**AMBER**    Well, that's just temporary. All I need is a building, a few thousand books, and some index cards.

**GORD**    Sweet Mother of God.

**AMBER**    Yes?

**GORD**    I.... Could we have your line please?

**AMBER**    Oh. Right. Sorry. He is Jesus.

**GORD**    Flawless as usual, Amber.

**FIONA**    Well, that's not fair.

**GORD**    What's not fair?

**FIONA**    She's memorized her lines.

**GORD**    No, Fiona, she's memorized one line. Three words.

**FIONA**    Teacher's pet.

**GORD**    Right. And we plunge ahead. Mary says her line. One more time please, Amber.

**AMBER**    He is Jesus.

GORD      And then Ebenezer Scrooge peers into the cradle like so.

          *GORD looks into the cradle and then says his line.*

Ah! An intelligent boy! A remarkable boy! You there? Joseph?

          *BOB doesn't answer.*

I say, you there? Joseph?!

BOB       That's me, right?

GORD      That's you, right.

BOB       I don't have a script.

AMBER     You can read off mine, Bob.

BOB       Thanks.

AMBER     Just sit a little closer.

          *BOB moves closer. AMBER holds the script away from BOB.*

A little closer.

          *BOB moves closer and AMBER holds the script further away.*

Tuck right in there.

BOB       That's okay. I can see it.

AMBER     Are you sure?

BOB       Yes.

AMBER     Good.

GORD      Amber?

AMBER     Yes?

GORD      Everything all right?

AMBER     Couldn't be better.

GORD      So you're all set?

AMBER     Ready Eddie.

GORD      Stupendous. And again. You there? Joseph? What's today my fine
fellow?

BOB       Today? Why Christmas Day.

GORD      And tell me about last night. Christmas Eve. How was it?

BOB       *(reading)* Well, Mamma in her kerchief and I in my cap had just
settled down for a long winter's nap. When out on the lawn there arose such
a clatter, I sprang from the bed to see what was the matter.

**GORD**     And Santa Claus enters. *(pause)* And Santa Claus enters. *(pause)* Howard?

**HOWARD**  *(off)* I'm standing by!

**GORD**     Yes, I know that. And you stood by marvellously. But now I would like you to enter.

**HOWARD**  *(off)* Good enough! Just say when!

**GORD**     Now! I want you to enter now!

**HOWARD**  *(off)* And in I come.

> *HOWARD enters. He has a papier-mâché Rudolph between his legs and he is riding him in.*

Ho! Ho! Ho! Merry Christmas! Whoa, Rudolph. Whoa!

**GORD**     Howard?

**HOWARD**  Yes, dear boy.

**GORD**     What are you doing?

**HOWARD**  I'm entering, as you requested.

**GORD**     Why are you sitting on Rudolph?

**HOWARD**  I'm riding him in.

**GORD**     No, Howard, you don't ride in on Rudolph. Santa doesn't ride his reindeer.

**HOWARD**  He doesn't?

**GORD**     No, they're not horses, Howard, and Santa is not a cowboy. He's not a wrangler. He's not a buckaroo. The reindeer pull his sleigh.

**HOWARD**  Oh. Well, that's a revelation.

**GORD**     It is, isn't it?

**HOWARD**  Yes. So I just walk in with the little fellow.

**GORD**     Yes.

**HOWARD**  He follows me in perhaps.

**GORD**     Exactly. He follows you in.

**HOWARD**  Understood. Shall we try it again?

**GORD**     Let's do.

**HOWARD**  Excellent.

> *HOWARD exits.*

**FIONA**    It's going quite well, isn't it?

**GORD**     Superbly. Just clipping along. Ready Howard?

**HOWARD**   *(off)* I'm standing by!

**GORD**   And Santa Claus enters.

>   *HOWARD enters, dragging Rudolph by the reins.*

**HOWARD**   Ho! Ho! Ho! Merry Christmas.

>   *He looks down at Rudolph who is just lying there.*

Whoa Rudolph! ...Whoa. *(to the others)* Hello. Rudolph tells me there's a little boy here who's celebrating his very first Christmas.

**AMBER**   He's right here, Santa Claus. Come closer.

**FIONA**   Yes, behold, Santa. He is the son of Gord.

**GORD**   God.

**FIONA**   What's that?

**GORD**   He's not the son of Gord. He's the son of God.

**FIONA**   Who is?

**GORD**   The baby.

**FIONA**   Oh.

**GORD**   So can you give me that again please, Fiona?

**FIONA**   Give you what?

**GORD**   Your line.

**FIONA**   Ah, most definitely. Yes, behold, Santa. He is the son of God. I don't know, Gordon. That doesn't sound right to me.

**GORD**   Well, that's what he is.

**FIONA**   And you're sure about that?

**GORD**   Yes. I read it somewhere.

**HOWARD**   We're learning a lot here today, aren't we?

**FIONA**   I should say we are.

**GORD**   And one more time, Fiona. Thank you.

**FIONA**   Yes, behold, Santa. He is the son of God.

**GORD**   And Joseph.

**FIONA**   What's that? He's the son of God and Joseph? That can't be right.

**GORD**   No, Fiona. I was just calling for Joseph's line.

**FIONA**   Oh. Well, that's a relief.

**HOWARD**   I should say it is.

**GORD**   Joseph? Please?

**BOB**     Right. Uh.... Good evening and thank you all for coming. My wife Mary and I are glad you could all make it here tonight. Right, Mary?

**AMBER**     That's right, Joseph. It's nice to see so many friendly faces in attendance. And I'd like to send a special shout-out to all you shepherds out there.

**BOB**     Wait a minute.

**GORD**     Now what's wrong?

**BOB**     So many friendly faces in attendance? A shout-out? What is this, a roast?

**GORD**     The line is fine. They're greeting the gathering throng. Welcoming their guests.

**FIONA**     What guests? *(looking at BOB)* Ah, a new face. *(she moves to BOB)* Hello there. *(shaking BOB's hand)* Fiona Putzle. Charmed, I'm sure.

**GORD**     Fiona, please! You've already met him!

**FIONA**     Oh feezle.

**HOWARD**     Gordon?

**GORD**     Yes, Howard?

**HOWARD**     *(looking at Rudolph lying there)* I think Rudolph has passed out.

**GORD**     He's papiermâché, Howard. Papiermâché doesn't pass out.

**HOWARD**     Sorry. I was in the moment.

**GORD**     I'm sure you were. And then Mary greets everyone and Joseph says.

**BOB**     *(reading)* Won't you all join us in the dining room for some snacks?

**GORD**     And off they go.

**BOB**     Dining room?

**GORD**     Yes. And off they go.

**BOB**     This is a stable. Where's the dining room?

**GORD**     It's just an excuse to get everyone offstage.

**BOB**     But the dining room?

**GORD**     Yes, the dining room, yes. And then they all exit.

*He begins flipping through his script.*

Then we have the second spirit. The boring spirit. What was Dickens thinking? Really. Then the third spirit. That's the scary spirit. We'll work on those two later. And then after that, I finish off the evening with a dramatic recitation that will most assuredly stop the show. Good then. We're on schedule.

**BOB**     Aren't you going to do your recitation?

**GORD**    Beg your pardon?

**BOB**     Your recitation. Aren't you going to practise it?

**GORD**    Not necessary.

**BOB**     Why not?

**GORD**    Because I know it. There's no point in practising it. The more I do it, the less spontaneous it will sound. It will sound tiresome. Uninspired. Which reminds me. Fiona?

**FIONA**   Yes?

**GORD**    Act better, dear.

**FIONA**   It's on my to-do list.

**GORD**    Thank you.

**AMBER**   And how was I, Gordon?

**GORD**    You were heaven on rye bread, as usual. All right, you know what? Let's take another short break and regroup, shall we? Hmm? Five minutes everyone! Thank you! *(calling off)* Les, I need the Aspirin! The large bottle!

   *GORD exits backstage.*

**HOWARD**  I thought you were wonderful, love.

**FIONA**   Did you?

**HOWARD**  Letter perfect. A joy to watch.

**FIONA**   Oh, thank you, Howard. And you were triumphant as well.

**HOWARD**  I was merely riding the coattails of your performance.

**FIONA**   Oh, Howard.

   *HOWARD and FIONA exit. HOWARD carries Rudolph. As they exit, HOWARD playfully pokes FIONA in the rear end with Rudolph. FIONA giggles at this.*

**AMBER**   So, Bob, what do you think of our little group?

**BOB**     Well...

**AMBER**   Kind of strange, aren't they?

**BOB**     Kind of, yes.

**AMBER**   You'll get used to it.

**BOB**     Do you think you'll have this show ready by tomorrow night?

AMBER     Well, it'll be tight but we've done it every other year. Everything's always rushed around Christmas.

BOB     Yeah, I know a bit about Christmas rushes.

AMBER     And we have to rehearse at night because we all have day jobs. Well, all except me.

BOB     No library. Right.

AMBER     So I have my days free. You know, like I'm free around lunchtime.

BOB     Uh-huh.

AMBER     And dinnertime.

BOB     Right.

AMBER     Yep. Free for dinner. No plans. Wide open.

BOB     So, what do the other folks do for a living?

AMBER     Uh, Gordon grows grapes, Fiona files folders, Les lays linoleum, and Howard has a Hoagie Hut.

BOB     ...What does Les do again?

AMBER     Lays linoleum.

BOB     Uh-huh.

AMBER     So, you said you're not from here. Are you just visiting?

BOB     Yes, I'm here on a job, but I really think I could do more good back home.

AMBER     When are you going back?

BOB     I don't know for sure. I guess it all depends.

AMBER     On what?

BOB     I don't even know that for sure.

AMBER     And where are you staying while you're here?

BOB     I'm staying at a bed and breakfast.

AMBER     Oh.

BOB     Yes, it's a true bed and breakfast. I have a cot in the kitchen.

AMBER     I'm free for breakfast too.

BOB     Pardon me?

AMBER     Nothing. I was just saying that I was free for breakfast if you ever wanted to grab some grub together. You know, break bread. Flip flapjacks.

BOB     Can I ask you something?

AMBER     Please. Anything. Ask away. Shoot.

**BOB**      What can I do to help here?

**AMBER**    Pardon me?

**BOB**      In Thithelville. What can I do here?

**AMBER**    You can buy me breakfast, charm the chinos off of me, woo me for a wee while, and we'll live happily ever after!!

**BOB**      ...No, I meant how can I help with this show?

**AMBER**    Oh. How painfully awkward.

**BOB**      Well?

**AMBER**    Well, I'm not sure I know what you mean, Bob.

**BOB**      Well, is there somethin' messed up here? Something that needs fixing?

**AMBER**    You mean besides Gordon being grumpy, Fiona forgetful, Howard hefty, and Les loquacious?

**BOB**      Loquacious?

**AMBER**    Long-winded.

**BOB**      Oh.

**AMBER**    No, thankfully I think things are thoroughly thuperb.

**BOB**      Uh-huh. Well, there must be something broke. And I've got to figure out what it is and I mean like fast.

> *GORD and FIONA enter, bickering.*

**GORD**     Fiona, I would love to give you as many lines as Amber, my love, but I'm afraid it might be too taxing on you.

**FIONA**    Too taxing how?

**GORD**     Your powers of recall. They aren't what they used to be. You have lapses.

**FIONA**    Lapses? Why that's preposterous! I'm every bit as...

**GORD**     Every bit as what?

**FIONA**    I forgot what I was going to say.

> *HOWARD enters.*

**HOWARD**   Gordon, I don't know if I can continue. I simply cannot breathe in this costume.

**GORD**     Well, perhaps if you skipped a meal once in a while, Howard.

**HOWARD**   What are you saying?

**GORD**     I'm saying there is only so much fabric in this town. We should try and save some for those who aren't as well insulated as yourself.

HOWARD    Are you saying I'm overweight?

GORD    I'm saying you drove past overweight six months ago. You are now bearing down on the village of obese.

HOWARD    Why, I've never been so insulted.

FIONA    I remember now!

GORD    Yes, Fiona?

FIONA    No, it's gone again.

GORD    You see, Fiona. This is why Amber has more lines than you. Her memory card's not full.

FIONA    Well, I think you favour the stoplight girl because she's pretty.

*GORD stares at FIONA.*

Well?

GORD    I'm waiting for you to say something that I disagree with.

AMBER    Now wait a minute, Fiona. I'm not getting by on my gorgeous girl-next-door good looks. I've got talent too, right Gordon?

GORD    Oh dear.

AMBER    Gordon?

GORD    *(calling offstage)* Les, is the break over yet?

AMBER    Gordon?

GORD    Les!

AMBER    Gordon, answer me. You think I've got talent, right?

GORD    Amber, truth be told, you couldn't act your way out of a soap bubble.

AMBER    What?!

GORD    It would take a miracle. It would make walking on water seem like a parlour trick. But you light up the stage, my sweet. You positively light it up!

AMBER    I've got a good mind to storm out of here this minute.

FIONA    So do I!

HOWARD    So do I!

GORD    No, please, this is just a misunderstanding. Please don't leave.

HOWARD    Why shouldn't we leave?

GORD    I was talking to Amber.

HOWARD    That does it!

**FIONA**     It most certainly does!

**HOWARD**   Fiona? Amber?

**FIONA**     *(to GORD)* Goodnight to you, sir!

**AMBER**     Goodbye, Gordon!

> *HOWARD, AMBER, and FIONA exit. HOWARD returns and takes the tray of donuts. He exits.*

**GORD**      Fine! Go ahead and leave! But know this. You'll never work in this town again! Never! Except for you, Amber! You can come back anytime you like!

> *LES enters.*

**LES**       Gord?

**GORD**      Yes?

**LES**       Gord?

**GORD**      Yes?

**LES**       Gord?

**GORD**      Yes!?

**LES**     .  *(pulling the headphone off of one ear)* Break's over.

**GORD**      Thank you, Les. But I'm afraid we're done for the evening.

**LES**       Done?

**GORD**      Yes. In fact, it looks like there will be no show at all this year.

**LES**       No show?

**GORD**      No show.

**LES**       How so?

**GORD**      How so?

**LES**       I'd like to know.

**GORD**      I gotta go.

> *GORD exits.*

**LES**       Oh no. No show? This can't be happening. *(to BOB)* You? Can't you do something about this?

**BOB**       About what?

**LES**       Well, you heard Gord. There might not be a show. What will the townsfolk do for entertainment this Christmas? How will they get in the Christmas spirit if we don't have a show for them? It will be the emptiethed Chrithmath Thisthelville hath ever exthperienthed.

**BOB**      Hey, I can't worry about that. I've got my own problems.

**LES**      Like what?

**BOB**      Like trying to figure out what I'm supposed to fix here?

**LES**      Ahhhh! *(calling to the backstage area)* All right everyone! That's a wrap! Lock it down!

> *LES exits.*

**BOB**      I have got to figure out what's wrong here!

> *BOB sits, frustrated.*

> *End Act One, Scene Two.*

## ACT TWO Scene One

*Time: The next evening. The night of the show.*

*Place: The rehearsal hall.*

*LES enters, followed by a children's choir. Not a big choir. It could be four children, or it could be ten. LES carries a clipboard.*

**LES**      All right, here we go. Right this way. Quickly now. Quickly. Very good. Everybody onstage. That's the idea. There you go. Now, tonight you will enter in exactly the same way, find your mark and begin singing. You are scheduled to open the show. That's if we have a show.

*GORD enters from the back of the theatre and makes his way onto the stage.*

**GORD**      Les?

**LES**      Ah. Gord. There you are.

**GORD**      Sorry, I went back to my dressing room to read over the best wishes notes that were sent to me.

**LES**      Oh. Did you get many?

**GORD**      None. Is the choir ready?

**LES**      All set.

**GORD**      Good. I shall address them then. Wish me luck. Children don't take to me for some reason. I don't know what it is.

**LES**      I can't imagine.

**GORD**      Yes, it positively baffles me too.

**LES**      I'm sure you'll be fine.

**GORD**      Well, here's hoping. *(to the choir)* Hello you little hobgoblins.

*The children back up, frightened.*

**LES**      Gord?

**GORD**      What?

**LES**      I would just address them as children.

**GORD**      Really?

**LES**      Yes. It's more general. Less personal.

**GORD**      Oh. All right then. Good thinking. Yes. *(to the choir)* Hello, children. Hello! You all look wonderful. Very Christmasy. Yes, a delightful looking group.

*Turns his back then speaks quietly to LES.*

How am I doing? Do you think they like me?

LES        I think they like you as much as anyone possibly could, Gord.

GORD        Excellent. *(to the children)* Yes, you look very Christmasy. You know what I'd like to do? I'd like to hang you all from my tree.

           *The children scream.*

LES        No, it's all right! It's all right. He just meant that you look like little Christmas tree ornaments, that's all. Cute little Christmas tree ornaments.

GORD        Yes, that's all I meant. Yes. *(to LES)* A skittish group, aren't they?

LES        Yes.

GORD        Anyway, children, just stand at ease and we'll get to you in a very brief moment. Thank you.

           *He begins to turn away and then speaks to one of the children.*

It's not polite to stare you know. Look away. Look away. *(to LES)* He's making faces at me.

LES        That's Mr. Binkins' boy. He's cross-eyed.

GORD        Oh. A handsome lad though. So, any sign of anyone else yet?

LES        Anyone else like who?

GORD        You know? The cast?

LES        Oh, yes. They just came in. They're standing in the wings.

GORD        Shhhh!

LES        Sorry. *(whispering)* They're standing in the wings.

GORD        Well I heard you the first time, didn't I?

LES        What?

GORD        When you said it loudly. I heard it then, didn't I?

LES        Oh. Right.

GORD        So, they've returned after all, have they? Yes, I knew they'd come crawling back.

LES        I think they drove.

GORD        Uh-huh. Now...

LES        I saw their van out front.

GORD        Right. Now...

LES        A Vauxhall.

           *GORD stares at LES.*

...Black Sapphire.

| GORD | Yes! Thank you. Now, remember. We play it cool. Aloof. |
| LES | I don't know what aloof means, Gord. |
| GORD | Cavalier. |
| LES | Still nothing, Gord. |
| GORD | Distant. Uncaring. Cold. |
| LES | Oh. Like you. |
| GORD | Precisely. Can you do that? |
| LES | I've learned from the master. |
| GORD | Good. A Vauxhall. All right, let's hear the choir then, shall we? |
| LES | Check. Choir, it's all yours. Quiet backstage, please! |

> *LES exits.*

| GORD | Merciful father. |

> *GORD takes a seat in the front row, or if no seat is available, off to the side somewhere. The choir begins by singing "O Come All Ye Faithful" or "Joy to the World." After their first words— either "O Come" or "Joy," GORD interrupts.*

Thank you! Perfect. Thank you very much! That's exactly what I'm looking for. Exactly!

> *LES enters.*

| LES | Gord? |
| GORD | Yes? |
| LES | Gord? |
| GORD | Yes? |
| LES | Gord? |
| GORD | Yes!! |
| LES | I think we should let the choir sing the entire song. |
| GORD | Why? |
| LES | Well, for practise. |
| GORD | Practise? It's a Christmas carol. How can you mess up a Christmas carol? |
| LES | Well, I think they'd like the practice anyway. And they did drive all the way in from Kamloopth. |
| GORD | From where? |

LES        Kamloopth. Forty miles east of here on the way to Thu Thaint
Marie.

GORD      Fine. Let them practise then.

LES        All right, here we go folks. Quiet backstage, please!

> *LES exits.*

GORD      There's no one back there! *(to the choir)* There's no one back there.
He has his headphones plugged into his…. Go ahead. Practise.

> *GORD sits. The choir sings their carol. The carol ends, there is
> applause, and GORD stands.*

Outstanding! Simply wonderful! Thank you.

> *The choir starts their second carol.*

Oh, there's more. How marvellous.

> *GORD sits and the choir sings their second carol. The carol ends
> and GORD stands.*

GORD      Brilliant! Absolutely top-notch. Thank you. Thank you so much.
It's nice to see someone who can actually take direction for a change. Now,
off you go. Back to Hobbitville or wherever you came from. Thank you.
Thank you so much.

> *LES enters.*

*(To LES and pointing to one of the children in the choir.)* Keep an eye on that
last one there. He looks shifty.

> *BOB, AMBER, FIONA, and HOWARD enter.*

BOB        Hey, Gordo.

GORD      Well, look who's here. As I live and breath.

LES        Gord?

GORD      Yes?

LES        Gord?

GORD      Yes?

LES        Gord?

GORD      Yes?!!

LES        *(He pulls the headset off of one ear.)* Look who's here.

GORD      Yes, I see. Well, thank heaven. Thank heaven above. I was worried
you weren't coming and we'd have no show tonight.

HOWARD  Well, we didn't want to let the townsfolk down, Gordon.

GORD      I was talking to Amber.

**HOWARD** *(to BOB)* You see that? There he goes again.

**FIONA** I've got a half a mind to storm out of here.

**GORD** Yes, my love, you do.

**FIONA** Do what?

**GORD** Have half a mind.

**FIONA** Well, I never!

**BOB** All right, calm down, Fiona. Don't go gettin' all skull and crossbones on me here, all right?

**FIONA** But did you hear what he just said to me?

**BOB** Yes, I did.

**FIONA** And what was it exactly? Refresh me.

**BOB** Fiona, just let it roll. Turn the other cheek. If you don't show any anger it takes the sting out of his insults. Believe me I know. I've insulted thousands of people over the years.

**GORD** So what's this, Bob? Are you the leader of the pack now?

**AMBER** Bob called and calmly coerced the cast into reconsidering.

**HOWARD** That's correct. Bob saved your bacon, mister. Right, Fiona?

**FIONA** No, I'm a vegetarian. I'll just have a salad thank you.

**GORD** So, tell me Bob. Why did you take it upon yourself to patch this mess up?

**BOB** Because I've been sent here to do a job and I can't do that job if you people don't put this show on tonight.

**GORD** And what job is that?

**BOB** I don't know. I haven't figured that part out yet. But I know it has something to do with this show.

**GORD** How very mysterious for you. All right, let's get to work then. We haven't got much time. Les, get set up for the top of the show.

**LES** Check. *(calling backstage)* All right, top of the show people. Let's go!

*LES exits.*

**GORD** The rest of you, get backstage and into your costumes. We've got forty-five minutes to the curtain. There we go. Scoot.

*No one moves.*

Off you go! Go on.

*No one moves.*

A little hustle.

> *No one moves.*

What? What is it now?

**BOB**    Well, we've got to lay down some ground rules first. Get our house in order.

**AMBER**    That's right.

**HOWARD**    That's right.

> *They look at FIONA. She doesn't respond.*

**BOB**    Fiona? Are you with us, sister?

**FIONA**    Who dropped this house on my sister?!

**BOB**    Oh brother.

**FIONA**    On my brother!

**BOB**    All right, Fiona. Thanks. Good.

**GORD**    Ground rules? I'm sorry, Bob, but you don't lay down the ground rules. I lay down the ground rules. I'm the director.

**BOB**    No, I'm afraid that's not going to work for us, Gordman.

**GORD**    Come again? It's not going to work for you?

**BOB**    That's what I said.

**GORD**    What exactly do you mean, it's not going to work for us? Who do you people think you are? Look at you. You came to me, a shapeless, unskilled splotch on the butt cheek of community theatre. And I moulded you. I turned you into the barely passable excuses for actors that you are today. You would be nothing without me. You hear? Nothing!

**BOB**    You know, you gotta step up your friendly game my man. You are gonna get nowhere if you keep jammin' us up like that. Right folks?

**HOWARD**    Yo, yo.

**AMBER**    True dat.

**FIONA**    Word.

**BOB**    Now, here's the story. First of all, Santa's going to be wearing a red suit.

**HOWARD**    That's right. I will not mock the good name of Santa Claus by wearing anything else.

**GORD**    Sorry, but that is impossible. I cannot consent to that.

**BOB**    All right, let's go folks.

> *BOB, AMBER, HOWARD, and FIONA turn to leave.*

| | |
|---|---|
| **GORD** | Wait! How about a red sash? |
| **BOB** | Howard? |
| **HOWARD** | No. |
| **GORD** | A red boutonniere? |
| **HOWARD** | No. |
| **GORD** | A red cummerbund? |
| **HOWARD** | No. The entire suit must be red. Top to bottom. |
| **GORD** | Fine. Santa will wear a red suit. Even if it is a cliché. |
| **BOB** | Good. Ya happy, Howard? |
| **HOWARD** | Completely. Thank you. |
| **BOB** | Secondly, you insulted Amber when you said she couldn't act her way out of a soap bubble. That was mean and hurtful, right Amber? |
| **AMBER** | I cried myself to sleep that night. Well, I do that every night, but still. |
| **BOB** | And so, that wrong must be put right. |
| **GORD** | Oh, here we go. What does she want? Damages? A cash settlement? |
| **BOB** | She wants an apology. |
| **GORD** | She wants what? |
| **BOB** | An apology. |
| **GORD** | An apology? That's it? |
| **BOB** | That's it. |
| **AMBER** | Sometimes a simple sorry is sufficient if it's sincere. |
| **GORD** | All right. I'm sorry, Amber. I'm sorry for what I said. |
| **AMBER** | Thank you. |
| **BOB** | Feel better now? |
| **AMBER** | Not really. I guess sometimes a simple sorry is sadly insufficient. Sufferin' succotash. |
| **BOB** | Number three. Fiona gets to play all three spirits. |
| **GORD** | She what? |
| **FIONA** | I what? |
| **BOB** | Past, present, and future. |
| **GORD** | Impossible. |

**BOB**     Why?

**GORD**     Because Fiona can't remember lines. To give her more would be catastrophic at this point.

**BOB**     What's to remember? The future dude doesn't say anything anyway.

**GORD**     No. It's out of the question. If she forgets a line she will be left standing out there with egg on her face. She'll embarrass herself. I'm sorry, Fiona, but I'm only doing this for your sake, love.

**BOB**     *(pulling GORD aside)* Gord, come on. Haven't you ever forgotten a line onstage?

**GORD**     Never.

**BOB**     Never?

**GORD**     Not once. I am a complete professional.

**BOB**     Hmm. So you won't let Fiona play all three spirits, huh?

**GORD**     She can't. It's beyond her means.

**BOB**     Okay, fine.

**GORD**     I'm glad you understand.

**BOB**     Oh, I understand. I understand that the audience is going to be awfully disappointed when they don't get a show tonight. See ya.

>          *BOB moves back towards the others.*

**GORD**     ...Wait. All right. Agreed.

**BOB**     Excellent.

**GORD**     But, I'm telling you right now, it will ruin the show. And it will be on your head.

**BOB**     Whatever. *(to FIONA)* Fiona, good news. You've got more lines now.

**FIONA**     I do?

**BOB**     You do.

**FIONA**     Oh that's wonderful. Thank you, Boob. I won't ever forget what you've done for me here.

**BOB**     I know you won't forget.

**FIONA**     Won't forget what?

**BOB**     And finally—and this is for everyone here—I know what it's like to work in a group situation. I've worked in a group situation for an eternity, and groups don't function properly—you know, they don't get their groove on—unless everyone works together. I mean, each group is made up of individuals, right? And each individual is different. And maybe because of these differences, maybe they don't get along. Maybe they're gettin' up in each other's faces all the time. For instance, let's say in your group you've got your Dinks *(points to HOWARD),* your Wieners *(points to FIONA),* and your Tools *(points to AMBER).* Now, maybe...

**HOWARD**  Wait. One moment.

**BOB**  What is it?

**HOWARD**  Can I be a Wiener?

**BOB**  What?

**HOWARD**  A Wiener. I'd rather be a Wiener than a Dink.

**BOB**  Why?

**HOWARD**  Well, I feel more like a Wiener than a Dink.

**BOB**  Fine. You're a Wiener. Fiona, you're a Dink.

**FIONA**  And I shall be a superb Dink.

**AMBER**  So what am I now?

**BOB**  You're still a Tool.

**AMBER**  I'm a Tool?

**BOB**  You're a Tool. Weiner, Dink, Tool. Got it?

**AMBER**  Got it.

**BOB**  Now, maybe the Dinks don't get along with the Tools. Maybe the Tools think they're better than the Wieners. Maybe the Wieners are dissin' on the Dinks. And why do these groups have these differences? Nobody knows. They've just been handed down from Wiener to Wiener. From Tool to Tool. That's right, from Dink to Dink. Maybe one has a different view on how a toy was created. Maybe one was raised in another part of town and talks the way people talk over in that part of town. Or maybe one wears a different coloured coat. A ridiculous, bright orange coat that makes them look like a traffic pylon. But you know what? We're not that different, no matter what part of town we come from. No matter what we believe. No matter what colour our coat is. And I think we can find love, understanding, and the spirit of co-operation if we just look in here. *(He points to his heart.)*

**FIONA**  In where, dear? In our shirt pockets?

**AMBER**  No, in our hearts.

**FIONA**  Oh, isn't that sweet?

**BOB**  Now, the Thithelville thitithens... citizens... are expecting a Christmas show tonight. They're counting on us to fill this hall with Christmas cheer. To put a seasonal smile of the face of every man, woman, and child among them. And are we gonna let them down?

> *AMBER, LES, HOWARD, and FIONA respond. No!*

Are we going to spoil their Christmas?

> *AMBER, LES, HOWARD, and FIONA respond. No!*

Gordo? It's up to you. What do you say?

**GORD**     What do I say? —I say let's get into our costumes and put on the best darned show Thithelville hath ever theen!!

> *AMBER, LES, HOWARD, and FIONA respond. Yay!*
>
> *GORD, LES, HOWARD, and FIONA exit.*

**AMBER**     Gee wallabies. That was inspiring, Bob.

**BOB**     Ya think so?

**AMBER**     It sure inspired me. It made me think "Wow, I want to do my best to get along with people, not just today, but every day of my life."

**BOB**     Good.

> *BOB starts to leave but AMBER grabs him by the arm and pulls him back.*

**AMBER**     I want to help people to understand one another. To understand and accept the many different cultures that we have in this world. I want people to put peace in perspective. Prioritize!

> *BOB takes out a hanky and wipes a bit of spit out of his eye.*

And once they do that, we can all live in harmony on this beautiful planet we call Earth.

**BOB**     That's terrific.

> *BOB starts to leave but AMBER grabs him by the arm and pulls him back again.*

**AMBER**     Yes, Bob, I want them to come into my library and read about the world's cultures. Learn more about them. And go away with a whole new appreciation of our fellow human beings.

**BOB**     But there is no library.

**AMBER**     Way to burst a bookworm's bubble, Bob.

**BOB**     Don't worry, Amber. You'll get your library one day. And you'll be the best darned librarian this side of Gwande Pwairie.

**AMBER**     You think so?

**BOB**     Absowutewy.

**AMBER**     Aw gosh, you're swell, Bob.

**BOB**     I think you're pretty swell too, Amber.

**AMBER**    Really?

**BOB**    Really.

**AMBER**    Gee, it's too bad you're not staying around for long. I think we could become the bestest friends.

**BOB**    Well, I really don't know how long I'm staying.

**AMBER**    No?

**BOB**    No, I might fail at what I was sent here to do and I might not be able to go home again. I might never see my friends again. The people I grew up with. Spent my whole life with. I'll be stuck here forever. Alone and miserable.

**AMBER**    Well, fingers crossed.

**BOB**    But I can't worry about that now. We've got an audience to think about. Come on, Amber. Let's go and put on a show.

**AMBER**    Right behind you, Bob!

**BOB**    After you.

**AMBER**    Right in front of you, Bob!

**BOB**    On with the show!

> *AMBER and BOB exit. The choir enters and sings a carol or two. The carol ends and GORD enters.*

**GORD**    Thank you, choir. Thank you very much. Lovely job. *(to the audience)* Weren't they wonderful? The choir is under the direction of Bernard Binkins. That's right, of Binkins' Grocery fame, where this week, cumquats are two for a dollar. And as I always say, you can never have too many cumquats. And just a reminder, on your way out of the theatre don't forget to peruse our seasonal lobby display provided by Binkins' Grocery. It's the history of tomato disease, entitled, O Holy Blight. This is even more riveting than last year's dairy display. You may recall that one. Curds and Whey in a Manger. Now, good evening and welcome to this year's Christmas tale presented by the Thithelville Thespians. We've entitled this year's show, "'Twas The Night Before a Christmas Carol in a Manger, Rudolph." The title is actually in your programs on pages two through five. Now, as our story opens it is a blustery, snowy Christmas Eve. *(pause)* I say it is a blustery and snowy Christmas Eve!

**LES**    *(off)* I'm on it, Gord! I need the wind, people!

> *We hear a wind sound effect.*

**GORD**    On this particular Christmas Eve, we are at the North Pole where Santa Claus and Tiny Tim are steeped in conversation. Let's listen in.

> *GORD exits. HOWARD as SANTA and AMBER as Tiny Tim enter. AMBER is on a crutch and wears a tattered hat. They are fighting an imaginary wind as they enter. The wind sfx stops.*

*AMBER and HOWARD stop fighting the wind and look around. Realizing the sfx has failed, HOWARD begins to speak. Throughout this next section, when AMBER speaks she changes hands with the crutch a few times, using it first under her left arm, and then under her right arm, etc.*

**HOWARD**  Ho! Ho! Ho! It certainly is blustery and snowy out here, Tim.

**AMBER**  It certainly is, Santa. I can barely stay righted.

**HOWARD**  So tell me something, Tiny. Can I call you Tiny?

**AMBER**  Can I call you Tubby?

**HOWARD**  All right then, Tim it is. Tell me something, Tim. If you could have one wish come true this Christmas—if you could have anything in the world—what would it be?

**AMBER**  Oh, golly Santa, that's easy. You see, my father, Bob Cratchet, doesn't make very much money so we're always wanting for something. My brothers and sisters don't have any money for school supplies like pencils and paper, so instead of taking notes, they press up against the blackboard after class and then go home and read the notes in the mirror. And my father walks to work every day and his shoes are worn right through to his stockings and yet he can't afford to have them cobbled, so each morning before he heads off to work, he stuffs his shoes with the local newspaper.

**HOWARD**  That's terrible.

**AMBER**  Oh, you've read it have you?

**HOWARD**  Yes.

**AMBER**  And my little baby brother doesn't have any baby food at all, so he has to eat what the grown-ups eat and those brussels sprouts make him awful gassy. And my mother has worn the same dress now for the past twenty-seven years. Twenty-seven years! But she never complains. Nope. She just keeps on wearing that dress even though it's threadbare and covered in soot.

**HOWARD**  Soot?

**AMBER**  From when she pops up to clean the chimney.

**HOWARD**  Oh.

**AMBER**  Yeah, she's a gamer all right. So, as you can see, Santa, we don't have very much at all. It's a struggle just to get through each day.

**HOWARD**  That's very sad indeed, Tim. So what would your wish be?

**AMBER**  I'd like a new hat.

**HOWARD**  A new hat?

**AMBER**  That's right. A more stylish lid.

**HOWARD**  Hmmm. That's awfully selfish, Tim.

AMBER    It is?

HOWARD   It most certainly is. Don't forget, it is better to give than to receive.

AMBER    Gee, you're right, Santa. Shame on me. Oh! I know. I know what I'd wish for. I'd wish for peace on earth.

HOWARD   Good boy!

AMBER    And a new hat.

HOWARD   Ho! Ho! Ho!

> *HOWARD and AMBER bow and exit. There is some sort of transition music to indicate a passage of time. GORD enters dressed as Ebenezer Scrooge.*

GORD     That night, Ebenezer Scrooge was visited by three spirits. The first being the Spirit of Christmas Past. The spirit took Mr. Scrooge on a long journey, way back in time, to a ramshackle stable on the evening of the very first Christmas.

> *FIONA enters dressed as the Spirit of Christmas Past.*

FIONA    Ebenezer Scrooge! I am the Spirit of Christmas Past!

GORD     *(surprised that FIONA got the line right)* That's right! I mean, yes you are, yes. And you have brought me to Bethlehem. I certainly enjoyed our stop at that grocery store on the way here. Binkins' I think it was called, where I bought a sandwich from their deli department. A tasty Bethleham and cheese. *(He looks to the heavens.)* Forgive me. *(to the audience)* Mr. Scrooge and the Spirit approached the manger. Slowly, reverently, and ever so humbly.

> *We hear a doorbell.*

AMBER    *(off)* Coming!

> *AMBER and BOB enter dressed as Mary and Joseph.*

Hi there! Come on in. You probably followed that bright star here, didn't you? Well, here's the reason that star was shining so brightly. Our son. Isn't he cute? Look, he's got his father's chin.

> *AMBER puts the baby in the cradle and BOB and AMBER sit.*

GORD     Spirit, what child is this?

FIONA    He is the King of Kongs, Mr. Scrooge.

GORD     King of Kings. He is the King of Kings.

FIONA    Well, at least I got your name right.

AMBER    He is Jesus.

GORD     *(He looks into the cradle.)* Ah! An intelligent boy! A remarkable boy! You there? Joseph?

**BOB**      Wazzup?

**GORD**     What's today, my fine fellow?

**BOB**      Today? Why Christmas Day.

**GORD**     And tell me about last night. Christmas Eve. How was it?

**BOB**      Well, Mamma in her kerchief and I in my cap had just settled down for a long winter's nap. When out on the lawn there arose such a clatter, I sprang from the bed to see what was the matter.

*HOWARD enters as SANTA Claus, riding Rudolph.*

**HOWARD**  Ho! Ho! Ho! Merry Christmas! Whoa, Rudolph! Whoa big fella!

*HOWARD climbs off of Rudolph and lets him drop to the floor; to the others.*

Howdy. Rudolph tells me there's a little pardner here who's celebrating his very first Christmas.

**AMBER**    He's right here, Santa Claus. Come closer.

**FIONA**     Yes, behold, Santa. He is the son of God and Joseph.

**BOB**      Good evening and thank you all for coming. My wife Mary and I are glad you could all make it here tonight. Right, Mary?

*AMBER is staring longingly at BOB.*

Right, Mary?

**AMBER**    I love you, Joseph.

**BOB**      ...Well, I hope so because we've just had a baby. Now, won't you all join us in the dining room for some snacks? Come. I think the dining room is in the east wing.

*BOB flashes a sarcastic look at GORD. HOWARD, FIONA, BOB, and AMBER move to exit*

**AMBER**    I love you, Joseph.

**BOB**      I heard you, Mary.

*BOB, AMBER, HOWARD, and FIONA exit.*

**GORD**     We skip ahead now, mercifully, to Scrooge's meeting with the Spirit of Christmas Yet to Come. We would love to show you the meeting with the second spirit, but we're running late and the manger has to be back to Betty's Bassinettes by ten. The meeting with the second spirit is boring anyway. You're not missing a thing. However, the visit from the third spirit wasn't nearly as uneventful.

*LES enters with a tombstone. He has trouble getting it through the entranceway. He puts it down and looks at it. Then he moves it slightly and looks at it. Then he moves it one more time and looks at it. He gives a thumbs-up to GORD.*

The third spirit was a foreboding spirit. Unfriendly and threatening. This spirit frightened Ebenezer. Shook him to his very foundation.

> *FIONA enters dressed as the Spirit of Christmas Yet to Come. She wears a hooded robe and she can't see very well out of it. She bangs into the doorway as she enters and then feels her way towards GORD.*

The spirit took Ebenezer to a churchyard which was littered with tombstones. It was here that the spirit hoped to give Scrooge a glimpse into his future and offer him one final chance to mend his ways.

> *We hear a loud clap of thunder. FIONA screams and throws her arms around GORD's neck. GORD releases himself from FIONA's grasp and continues.*

In the churchyard the Spirit stood among the graves and pointed down to one.

> *Pause. FIONA does not point.*

I said the Spirit stood among the graves and pointed down to one.

> *Pause. Still no pointing.*

Fiona?

**FIONA**   Yes, love.

**GORD**   Point.

**FIONA**   I beg your pardon?

**GORD**   Point. Point!

**FIONA**   Point at what?

**GORD**   A grave.

**FIONA**   Where are they? I can't see.

**GORD**   Just point anywhere.

> *FIONA points straight out, across GORD's face. GORD takes her arm and points it down to the tombstone.*

"Before I draw nearer to that stone to which you point, answer me one question. Are these the shadows of the things that will be, or are they the shadows of the things that may be only?" The spirit did not answer.

**FIONA**   Things that may be only.

**GORD**   Except for one brief, unscripted sentence. "Good Spirit, assure me that I yet may change these shadows you have shown me by an altered life. I promise I will honour Christmas in my heart and try to keep it all the year."

**FIONA**   It's a deal.

GORD        What?

FIONA       It's a deal. I assure you.

GORD        No, the spirit doesn't assure anybody. The spirit doesn't speak.

FIONA       But it's hot inside this costume. I have to get offstage.

GORD        The scene's not over yet.

FIONA       No, I have to leave. I feel faint. I'm gonna pass out.

GORD        All right. Fine. Go.

>           *FIONA turns and moves towards the wings with her hands*
>           *outstretched because she can't see.*

And so the Spirit left the graveyard as swiftly and as quietly as he had appeared.

FIONA       I'm melting! Oh, what a world. What a world!

>           *FIONA bumps into the wall and then finally manages to get*
>           *offstage. GORD goes behind the wall and sticks his head out*
>           *the window.*

GORD        And looking down from his bedroom window, Ebenezer Scrooge
called out to the four wise men. "Come back with the man and I'll give you
a shilling. Come back with him in less than five minutes, and I'll give you
half a crown!" And off they went to buy the turkey. From Binkins' Grocery.
Where the fowl is always fair. And along their journey they were guided by
Rudolph and his shiny red nose. And this was very encouraging for
Rudolph. You see, up until now, he didn't feel as though he belonged
because all of the other reindeer wouldn't let Rudolph join in any reindeer
games. They rejected him.

>           *LES enters with the papier-mâché Rudolph and slides it across*
>           *the floor towards GORD's window. LES exits. GORD looks*
>           *down at Rudolph.*

With extreme prejudice. And Scrooge was better than his word. He did alter
his life. He did all that he promised and infinitely more. And he became a
second father to Tiny Tim who did not die.

>           *AMBER enters dressed as Tiny Tim.*

AMBER       It's a miracle, Mr. Scrooge. I did not die.

GORD        Yes, Tim. I can see that.

AMBER       Yes, a true miracle. I can walk. I can run! And I can act my way out
of a soap bubble!

>           *AMBER does a quick tap-dance step.*

GORD        Yes, that is a true miracle indeed. *(to the audience)* Scrooge had
no...

*AMBER waves to someone in the audience.*

What are you doing?

**AMBER**     I'm waving to my sister.

**GORD**     Jasmine from Jasper?

**AMBER**     Mindy from Minsk.

**GORD**     May I continue?

**AMBER**     Rock on.

**GORD**     Thank you. *(to the audience)* Scrooge had no further interaction with the Spirits, but lived on the total abstinence principle ever afterwards. And it was always said that he knew how to keep Christmas well, if any man alive possessed the knowledge. May that truly be said of all of us. And so, as Tiny Tim observed...

**AMBER**     God bless us every one.

*AMBER picks up Rudolph and exits.*

**GORD**     Ladies and gentlemen, we have reached the point in this year's pageant where I perform my annual soliloquy. I know how much you look forward to this part of the program each and every year and I only hope that once again I can live up to your great expectations. For I am your humble servant, here to please. And so without further adieu...

*He clears his throat and begins.*

And then in a twinkling, I heard on the roof, the prancing and pawing of each little hoof. As I drew in my head and was turning around, down the chimney St. Nicholas came with a bound. He was dressed all in fur from his head to his foot, and his clothes were all tarnished with ashes and soot. A bundle of toys he had flung on his back, and he looked like a peddler just opening his pack.

*He pauses. He's forgotten his line.*

He was.... Uh... he was.... Uh.... Oh dear. Uh... he was...

*BOB enters.*

**BOB**     He was chubby and plump, a right jolly old elf,
And I laughed when I saw him, in spite of myself!
A wink of his eye and a twist of his head,
Soon gave me to know I had nothing to dread.

*AMBER enters.*

**AMBER**     He spoke not a word, but went straight to his work, And filled all the stockings, then turned with a jerk.

*LES enters.*

LES     And laying his finger aside of his nose,
        And giving a nod, up the chimney he rose!

        *FIONA enters.*

FIONA   He sprang to his sleigh, to his team gave a whistle,
        And away they all flew like the down of a thistle.
        But I heard him exclaim, 'ere he drove out of sight,

        *HOWARD enters.*

HOWARD  Happy Christmas to all, and to all a good night!

GORD    And so ends our Christmas tale for another year. The Thithelville Thespians would like to thank you all very much for coming. And I would personally like to thank them, each and every one of them, for their hard work and for their unflagging dedication. They have truly shown me what the spirit of Christmas is all about and it is the greatest gift I could have received. God bless us every one!

        *Everyone exits.*

        *End Act Two, Scene One.*

## ACT TWO Scene Two

        *Time: The next day.*

        *Place: SANTA's office.*

        *Lights come up. We hear music. SANTA is dancing. BOB enters.*

SANTA   Bob, you're back!

BOB     Yes, and you're dancing.

SANTA   That's right. I'm bustin' a move.

BOB     And probably a floorboard or two as well.

SANTA   So Bob, how was the trip home?

BOB     Cool.

SANTA   Good.

BOB     No, I mean it was cool. As in cold. I froze my tookus. You gotta put a roof on that sleigh, Santa.

SANTA   Oh no, Bob. I enjoy the fresh air. It puts colour in my cheeks! Makes me look cute and cuddly.

BOB     Right. Well, anyway, thanks for sending the sleigh for me. I was worried that you were gonna forget about me.

SANTA     No, I wouldn't do that, Bob. Never. You're my favourite elf.

BOB     I am?

SANTA     No, of course not. I'm just having fun with you. I don't have any favourites. You're all my favourites.

BOB     Oh.

SANTA     So tell me, Bob. I can't wait to hear the news. What did you learn in Thithelville?

BOB     Well, Santa, I'll be honest...

SANTA     Oh I hope so, Bob. In fact, I insist on it. You see, honesty is a quality I expect from my elves because there is nothing to be gained from fibbing. I mean, you tell one fib and that leads to a little white lie. And that little white lie leads to a bigger lie and then an even bigger lie. And before long, nobody will believe a word you say because you've lied to them so often. No, always tell the truth, Bob. Always.

BOB     Are you done?

SANTA     I just thought this story should have a message of some kind.

BOB     Right.

SANTA     You can't do a Christmas show and not have a message.

BOB     Uh-huh. So, as I was saying, I don't think I learned a darn thing in Thithelville.

SANTA     No?

BOB     Not a thing. In fact, I don't see what the point of my going there was.

SANTA     So, you learned nothing?

BOB     Zip.

SANTA     Hmm. Well, that's disappointing. How did the show go?

BOB     Well, the show went fine once everybody pulled together and stopped bickering amongst themselves. You should have been there, Santa. They couldn't get along at all. And the complaints? I don't have enough lines; my Santa suit is too small; I don't have a library. It was endless.

SANTA     And how did it get fixed?

BOB     Well, I had to step in and lay down the law, Santa. I had to go buff. Get all Chuck Norris on 'em. You know, like you do sometimes. Yeah, I had to tell them that the group is only as strong as it's weakest link, and nothing ever gets accomplished unless you work together.

SANTA     Really?

BOB     Yep.

| SANTA | Hmm. So you learned nothing there? |
|-------|-------------------------------------|
| BOB | Not a thing. Now can I get back to work? |
| SANTA | Not just yet. I've got a little surprise for you. |
| BOB | What's that? |
| SANTA | Gordon?! |

*GORD enters.*

| GORD | Yes, Santa? |
|------|-------------|
| BOB | What? What's he doing here? |
| SANTA | Oh, Gordon and I are old friends. I always call on Gordon when I've got a special request. |
| BOB | What kind of special request? |
| SANTA | Gordon, how do you think Bob did? |
| GORD | He did very well, Santa. He was a little slow to get with the program, but he came through when it counted. He pulled everyone together and saved the show. |
| SANTA | Excellent. You hear that, Bob? You saved the show. |
| BOB | I did? |
| SANTA | You most certainly did. |
| BOB | Hmm. So, Gordo was on the inside? He was working for you? |
| SANTA | He most certainly was. But wait. There's more. Fiona? Les? |

*FIONA and LES enter.*

| BOB | What's going on here? |
|-----|-----------------------|
| FIONA | Hello, Bob. Fiona Putzle. Charmed, I'm sure. |

*FIONA shakes BOB's hand.*

| BOB | You remember me? |
|-----|------------------|
| FIONA | Of course I remember you. |
| SANTA | Fiona's as sharp as a tack, Bob. Mind like a steel trap. |
| FIONA | Thank you, Santa. |
| BOB | So the forgetful thing was just an act? |
| FIONA | What forgetful thing? |
| BOB | Well, when you couldn't... |
| FIONA | Gotcha again! |
| SANTA | Fiona, do you think Bob proved himself to everyone? |

| | |
|---|---|
| **FIONA** | He certainly did, Santa. You led by example, Bob. You showed us all that a little co-operation and graciousness go a long way. |
| **LES** | Bob? |
| **BOB** | Yes? |
| **LES** | Bob? |
| **BOB** | Yes? |
| **LES** | Bob? |
| **BOB** | Yes?!! |
| **SANTA** | That's my favourite! I love that! |
| **LES** | Thanks, Santa. |
| **SANTA** | What did you think of Bob, Les? |
| **LES** | Well, Santa, I'll be honest... |
| **SANTA** | Oh, I hope so, because there is nothing to be gained from fibbing. I mean, you tell one fib and that leads to a little white lie... |
| **BOB** | Santa? Chill, okay? *(to LES)* Go ahead, my man. You were saying? |
| **LES** | Well, Santa, Bob was a little on the rude side at first. |
| **SANTA** | Is that so? |
| **LES** | But when the chips were down, when the pressure was on, when push came to shove, when he was caught between a rock and a Vauxhall... |
| **SANTA** | Les? |
| **LES** | He did good, Santa. He did very good. |
| **SANTA** | You see that, Bob? You were a positive influence because you showed everyone how to work together. |
| **BOB** | Wow. |
| **SANTA** | So do you get it now? |
| **BOB** | Get what? |
| **SANTA** | The lesson you learned? |
| **BOB** | Sorry, Santa. I'm drawin' a blank. |
| **SANTA** | All right. Let's try this then. Amber? |
| | *AMBER enters.* |
| **AMBER** | Hi, Bob. |
| **BOB** | Hi. |
| **AMBER** | It's nice to see you again. |

BOB  It's nice to see you too.

AMBER  I've missed you.

BOB  I've been gone for three hours.

AMBER  Don't remind me.

BOB  Okay, wait a minute. Wait. I think I'm getting it now. *(to SANTA)* It was all a setup, right?

SANTA  Yes.

BOB  And they were all in on it?

SANTA  Every one of them.

BOB  So Gordo's not a jerk?

SANTA  No.

BOB  Fiona's not a ditz?

SANTA  No.

BOB  Les is not a pest?

SANTA  No.

BOB  Amber doesn't have a crush on me?

SANTA  No.

AMBER  Not so fast, Santa.

SANTA  All right, maybe I jumped the gun on that one.

BOB  What about Howard? Where's Howard?

SANTA  Howard? Well, let's see now. I'm standing by!

BOB  You? That was you?

SANTA  Yes, Bob. That was me.

BOB  So, all of that overeating, that was just an act?

SANTA  What overeating?

BOB  Never mind.

SANTA  You see, Bob, this was an elaborate plan designed to teach you a lesson.

BOB  You mean you care that much about me, Santa, that you would go to all this trouble just to get me back on track?

SANTA  Well, I think you're worth it, Bob. Yes, everybody has a basic goodness in them, my friend. You just have to look for it sometimes. I knew I'd find your good side if I looked long and hard enough.

BOB  Wow. I'm blown away.

| SANTA | So do you understand now? Are you with it? Are you hip to the be bop shoo op? |
|---|---|
| BOB | Excuse me? |
| SANTA | Do you finally get it? |
| BOB | Oh, do I ever get it! It's obvious! |
| SANTA | Wonderful! |
| BOB | It was all planned to teach me a lesson. |
| SANTA | Exactly! |
| BOB | ...So, what was the lesson? |
| SANTA | Oh dear. |
| AMBER | Never mind, Santa. I'll brief Bob on the be bop shoo op at the bowling alley. |
| SANTA | Well said. Now what night is this, everybody? |
| ALL | Christmas Eve! |
| SANTA | It most certainly is. And what do I do on Christmas Eve? |
| ALL | Deliver the toys to the girls and boys! |
| SANTA | Exactly! But first... we dance! |
| BOB | Oh, Santa, no. |
| SANTA | Oh, I'm afraid so, Bob. Les? Music please! |
| LES | Right away, Santa. *(calling offstage)* Cue the music, people! |
| GORD | Who are you talking to? There's no one back there. |

*Music starts.*

Well, I'll be a monkey's uncle.

*Everyone but BOB begins to dance.*

| SANTA | Come on, Bob! |
|---|---|
| BOB | Ah, what the heck. |

*BOB begins to dance. Lights down.*
*End.*

*Photo by Jacquline Foster*

**Norm Foster** has been called Canada's pre-eminent comic playwright, and he is also one of the most prolific and most produced of all Canadian playwrights. *Halifax Chronicle-Herald* columnist Ron Foley writes "Foster's stage writing remains one of Canada's greatest theatrical treasures," and *The Calgary Herald* describes him as "one of the funniest writers of intelligent comedy in Canadian theatre today." Mr. Foster has more than forty plays to his credit. He is the recipient of the Los Angeles Drama-Logue Award for his play *The Melville Boys* and has been honoured with an award from Theatre Ontario for his "distinguished service to Ontario's theatre community."